Modern Warfare

PSI Classics of the Counterinsurgency Era

Counterinsurgency Warfare: Theory and Practice
David Galula

Communist Revolutionary Warfare: From the Vietminh to the Viet Cong
George K. Tanham

Modern Warfare: A French View of Counterinsurgency
Roger Trinquier

Counter-Guerrilla Operations: The Philippine Experience
Napolean D. Valeriano and Charles T.R. Bohannan

MODERN WARFARE

A French View of Counterinsurgency

Roger Trinquier

Translated from the French by Daniel Lee
With an Introduction by Bernard B. Fall

Foreword by Eliot A. Cohen

PSI Classics of the Counterinsurgency Era

Praeger Security International
Westport, Connecticut • London

Library of Congress Cataloging-in-Publication Data

Trinquier, Roger.

  Modern warfare : a French view of counterinsurgency / Roger Trinquier; Translated from the French by Daniel Lee; With an introduction by Bernard B. Fall; Foreword by Eliot A. Cohen.

    p. cm. — (PSI Classics of the Counterinsurgency Era)

  Includes bibliographical references and index.

  ISBN 0–275–99267–5 (alk. paper) – ISBN 0–275–99268–3 (pbk : alk. paper)

  1. Tactics 2. Guerrilla warfare 3. Subversive activities 4. France —Defenses I. Title II. Series

UA700.T713 1964

355   64013363

British Library Cataloguing in Publication Data is available.

Library of Congress Catalog Card Number: 64013363
ISBN: 0–275–99267–5
    0–275–99268–3 (pbk.)

First published in France in 1961 under the title *La Guerre Moderne* by Editions de la Table Ronde

Praeger Security International, 88 Post Road West, Westport, CT 06881
An imprint of Greenwood Publishing Group, Inc.
www.praeger.com

Printed in the United States of America

The paper used in this book complies with the Permanent Paper Standard issued by the National Information Standards Organization (Z39.48–1984).

10 9 8 7 6 5 4 3 2 1

CONTENTS

FOREWORD

World War II divided the French military and the experience of bitter conflicts in Indochina and Algeria did so again—culminating in one successful and one unsuccessful revolt by the military against the government. Roger Trinquier was no Gaullist: an officer in the colonial infantry, he spent the war first defending the French concession in Shanghai and then in Indochina under the Japanese occupation. Yet although he missed fighting with the Free French in North Africa and Europe or with the *maquis*, he saw plenty of action during the rest of his career. Following his internment by the Japanese in 1945, he continued to serve in Indochina and then in Algeria.

He led counterguerrilla units against the Viet Minh, including thousands of montagnard tribesmen in the climactic battle of Dien Bien Phu; narrowly escaping being purged as a Vichy sympathizer, he rotated between training assignments in France and duty as a paratrooper in Algeria, including with the 10th Parachute Division under General Jacques Massu during the Battle of Algiers in 1957. He commanded a regiment on the Tunisian border and after that, luckily for him, was in Greece drawing up plans for operations in the Congo when his friends and former superiors launched an abortive coup against President Charles de Gaulle in 1961. But his days of soldiering were over, and a moderately successful years as a writer began.

Modern Warfare is the book which made his mark among English speaking readers, and deservedly so. It is the product of a great deal of experience with counterinsurgency operations. Indeed, it is worth noting that in over a thirty-year career in the army he spent all of it engaged in irregular warfare. Promotion was not rapid: sixteen years after receiving his commission he was a deputy battalion commander in Indochina; and at its end he was only a regimental commander. But like many of his peers, he acquired a rare depth of experience and perhaps something more: the perspective that comes to those who have waged war in two distinct political eras. Much of the interest in this book comes from his realization that the petty war against bandits and rebels of the pre-1939 period had changed forever as a result of World War II.

For Trinquier, the enemy—here referring primarily to the Algerian insurgents—means a nationalist totalitarian type, utterly different from indigenous enemies of earlier years. What the new insurgent brings to war is not merely ideological zeal or deep felt resentment, but technique and discipline. Trinquier makes dissection of that technique his point of departure. His account of bomb-making cells, compartmentalized hierarchies, and how the use terror remain as valid as they were half a century ago. Indeed, in some respects the Algerian insurgents, and earlier their Vietnamese counterparts, were more sophisticated than some of the groups active today.

The French theorists of revolutionary war, Trinquier among them, saw these struggles as a contest for the political mobilization of a normally inert populace. Familiar with the work of communist movements in Europe, they understood the role of front organizations, and assigned importance to trade unions and teachers, among others, as well as the establishment of social institutions that would gradually erode legitimacy and efficacy from the government. A parallel insurgent leadership that would undo by night what the authorities could did in daylight. The battlefields were webs of social life, and not just along jungle trails or dried riverbeds.

For this enemy Trinquier has the cold respect of a professional warrior. He describes an enemy who is deeply committed to his cause, and ingenious in its pursuit. One knows, without being aware of Trinquier's combat record, that he would probably give little quarter to an enemy whom he could not turn or exploit in some other way. But there is no cultural condescension here, nor anything but respect for the courage of those he is committed to fight.

What of Trinquier's technique? The book has gained some notoriety for the passage in which he discusses, obliquely but clearly enough, the use of torture. The terrorist "claims the same honors [as the soldier] while rejecting the same obligations." But the forces of order, Trinquier insists, cannot treat the captured terrorist as a criminal (who acts not out of personal motives or greed) nor as a soldier. He must be quickly interrogated and, in several chilling lines, the author describes what ensues:

> No lawyer is present for such an interrogation. If the prisoner gives
> the information requested, the examination is quickly terminated; if not,

specialists must force his secret from him. Then, as a soldier, he must face the suffering, and perhaps the death, he has heretofore managed to avoid. The terrorist must accept this as a condition inherent in his trade and in the methods of warfare that, with full knowledge, his superiors and he himself have chosen.

Unsurprisingly, this and similar passages have given Trinquier a reputation for justifying the use of torture. There is much to criticize: he does not reflect on what using such methods do to those who inflict as well as those who undergo torture nor consider the doubtful validity of information extracted under physical duress. He assumes torture can be applied clinically and with restraint, and he seems oblivious to the political damage done by widespread use of these means. Perhaps the best that what can said is that he considers—albeit not thoroughly—a horrible issue.

On the other hand, Trinquier is quick to add that after interrogation terrorists should be treated like normal prisoners of war, and he compares modern insurgents to members of the French resistance accepting the risks of fighting the Germans outside the laws of war, tacitly ceding considerable moral stature to insurgents. He repeatedly insists on the importance of treating the population who constitute the battleground of irregular warfare with consideration and respect. And perhaps most importantly of all, physical coercion is quite clearly only a part of what he thinks counterinsurgency is all about.

Indeed, Trinquier's justification of torture has caused much of what is valuable or at least interesting about this book to be ignored—in particular his discussion of the need for what today is called clear-and-hold operations, for countermobilization of the local population to conduct espionage as well as resistance, for the comparison of counterinsurgency in urban and rural environments. On all these points he is instructive, and one can only wish that, for example, American commanders going to Iraq would have understood as he did the importance of such measures as the use of national identity cards or, conversely, the futility of such measures as large-scale sweeps through insurgent areas, inaccurate aerial bombing, or hunkering down in fortified bases separated from the population they are seeking to protect.

Modern Warfare is not a detached treatise—or rather only in part. It boldly challenged complacent senior military leaders who the author believed did not fully understand the threat. Trinquier's indictment of the French army is severe: he believes that conventional soldiers are uninterested and uninformed about a form of warfare in which tactical problems are limited, in which force is a small proportion of effective action, and in which local political considerations play the dominant role. He and other

French officers with similar experience knew how costly such attitudes could prove.

The U.S. military, both wrongly and unprofessionally, expressed contempt toward their French counterparts in the 1950s and 1960s. They themselves stumbled no less badly on many of the same battlefields in Southeast Asia. Americans turned aside from thinking about this kind of conflict after Vietnam, preparing for the war they preferred—massive, violent, and utterly conventional. For them, and not only for his own comrades, Trinquier's final warning bears reflection: "The nation does not ask the army to define problems, but to win the war it is engaged in." His path through the counterinsurgency era may not be ours, but this concentrated reflection on his travels and those of his comrades are well worth reading.

Eliot A. Cohen
May 2006

Eliot A. Cohen is Robert E. Osgood Professor of Strategic Studies in the Paul H. Nitze School of Advanced International Studies at the Johns Hopkins University and the author of *Supreme Command: Soldiers, Statesmen, and Leadership in Wartime.*

INTRODUCTION: A PORTRAIT
OF THE "CENTURION"

In a book that became one of France's greatest best sellers since World War II, Jean Lartéguy gave the name of "centurion" to the hard-bitten French regular who had survived the Indochina war, had learned his Mao Tse-tung the hard way, and later had sought to apply his lessons in Algeria or even in mainland France.[1]

Of that centurion—as the reader no doubt knows, this was the title of the company commanders who formed the backbone of the Roman Legions—Lartéguy says: "I shall always feel attached to those men, even if I should ever disagree with the course they choose to follow, [and] dedicate this book to the memory of all the centurions who perished so that Rome might survive."

Rome, of course, did *not* survive in its ancient splendor in spite of the incredible sacrifices of the centurions, nor did France survive as a world-wide empire. But in the case of France, the centurion exists as a live human being; right at this moment, he is either emerging from colonelcy to general's rank, or being placed on the compulsory retirement list—or, perhaps, being sentenced to the jails of the French Republic for Secret Army activities. For at least another decade, he and his kind are likely to exert a strong influence upon French military thinking and planning and, therefore, upon the Western alliance as a whole.

The French Army officer, to a far greater extent than his British-American counterpart, has spent the last quarter of a century fighting desperate rear-guard actions against highly politicized irregulars. In addition, the lack of coherent political leadership from Paris in the chaotic years of the Fourth Republic left the French military with a heavy burden of making political decisions at every level. Local commanders, for example, had to make the decision whether or not to arm local levies and if so, of what political or religious persuasion. In Indochina, such officers—often of captain's rank or lower—raised Catholic, Buddhist, Cao-Dai, Hoa-Hao, or mountain tribal militia forces whenever they did not use outright river pirates or deserters from the Communists. In return for such military assistance by the natives, those officers undertook *political* commitments of a far-reaching nature: They swore solemn oaths to protect either a given group from Communist reprisals or a given territory whose population had committed itself to them. From a purely tactical involvement, the war (both in Indochina and Algeria, but even more in the latter) became a highly personal involvement. An officer who would, under normal circumstances, have abandoned a given position for tactical reasons felt compelled to hold it because he himself had "promised" to hold it—and promised not his own superiors, but the people among whom he fought.

To withdraw became not only proof of military failure, but—and this above all—a blemish on one's personal honor as an "officer and a gentleman." To the Anglo-American mind, which sees its officers as Colonel Blimps and General Jubilation T. Cornpones (or their real-life counterparts of the retired extreme right-wing variety), this view of war seems inconceivable. And it is, of course, inconceivable in conventional war, where it is perfectly permissible to lose or win a terrain feature without losing one's military honor. The "I shall return" of General MacArthur amply redeemed the surrender of Corregidor; the Inchon landing, the bloody retreat to Pusan beachhead. But in such conventional wars (Trinquier calls them "traditional," to emphasize their obsoleteness), military operations go on without regard for the hapless civilian population. No one asks it to take sides in the struggle—at any rate, not at first, while the battle rages.

In revolutionary war (or, as Trinquier calls it throughout the book, italicizing the term for emphasis, *"modern warfare"*), the allegiance of the civilian population becomes one of the most vital objectives of the whole struggle. This is indeed the key message that Trinquier seeks to impress upon his reader: Military tactics and hardware are all well and good, but they are really quite useless if one has lost the confidence of the population among whom one is fighting.

And Roger Trinquier is extremely well qualified to write on this subject, for his own background makes him the perfect example of the scholarly warrior of peasant stock that is a vanishing breed in the other Western armies. (In all likelihood, Communist China's armies still have a few in their ranks, not the least of whom is Mao Tse-tung.) Trinquier was born in 1908 in La Beaume, a small mountain village in the French Alps where he still owns a home and spends his vacations. Until the age of thirteen, he went to the one-room village school. Because he was a bright student, his parents directed him toward what was then the most obvious path to social betterment for the son of a poor farmer—schoolteaching. He successfully passed the entrance examinations to the Normal School of Aix-en-Provence and graduated at the age of twenty, ready for a lifetime of teaching in the back country of southeastern France.

But like all other Frenchmen his age, he first had to put in his two years of compulsory military service. Since it is still a French saying that the schoolteachers make up the backbone of the French Army's reserve officers' corps, it was not surprising that Trinquier was sent to Reserve Officers' School. Although most schoolteachers consider their military career a necessary evil, Trinquier thought it a revelation of a vaster, more active world. He requested a transfer to the Officers' School of Saint-Maixent, then graduated, in 1931, into the French Marine Infantry; and since the French Marines (they were known as "Colonials" from 1870 until 1961, but have now taken on their old name again) were specifically trained for overseas duty, the young lieutenant soon found himself on a trip to the Far East.

His first assignment, as was the rule then, was probably his toughest: He found himself in command of an outpost at Chi-Ma, in the wildest and most isolated part of the Sino-Tonkinese border region, aptly called the "One Hundred Thousand Mountains," fighting Chinese pirates and opium smugglers. To stay alive there, one had to rely on native help, and Trinquier quickly learned how to find it. He also learned some of the mountaineer dialects. Upon his return to France in 1937, he was picked for another delicate assignment, as a member of the French Marine force guarding the International Concession in Shanghai, where Japan's aggression had just unleashed World War II. Trinquier was then reassigned to the command of one of the two Marine companies guarding the French Embassy in Peking. Other major powers—the United States, Britain, Italy, and Japan—also had units in the diplomatic enclave. Trinquier became very friendly with the American commander, Colonel Marstone, and he also learned Chinese.

When World War II officially broke out in Europe, in September, 1939, Trinquier was transferred back to Shanghai as deputy to the French battalion commander there. Pearl Harbor and its aftermath created an anomalous situation: Although the British and American units in Shanghai were disarmed and interned by the Japanese, the French—because they were under the nominal control of the Vichy Government in German-occupied France—were left unmolested and fully armed. The Japanese, however, did not trust the Vichy forces indefinitely; having overwhelmed them in Indochina, on March 9, 1945, they did likewise in Shanghai on the following day, whereupon Trinquier got a taste of Japanese imprisonment. (The existence of the French units in China was to lead, in at least one instance, to a rather comical situation after V-J Day: When American Marines in full battle gear went ashore near Tientsin, they were greeted by a French Marine detachment that presented arms to them. It was part of the nearby Peking garrison that had picked up its weapons again after the Japanese surrender.)

Promoted to the rank of captain in 1942 by the Vichy Government, Trinquier, like most of his comrades in neighboring Indochina, neither broke with Vichy nor sought to join General de Gaulle's Free French Forces—a fact that was later to affect his career decisively. His promotions were to come slowly, and the mutual distrust (more often, dislike) between the Free French officers and those who, though sympathetic to the Allied cause, had remained faithful to their soldier's oath—or so they were to rationalize it—never quite disappeared. It explains Trinquier's strong animosity toward de Gaulle, which he does not bother to hide and which comes through quite clearly in his political statements.

Liberated from the Japanese after V-J Day, Trinquier, like many of his comrades, sought an assignment in Indochina—perhaps as a demonstration that his wartime allegiance was dictated by motives other than fear of battle. Arriving in Saigon on January 3, 1946, he became a platoon commander in the commando group of Major Ponchardier, which had been given the difficult task of clearing Vietminh elements out of the swamps and rice paddies surrounding the city. Upon his return to France, however, Trinquier learned that, like other officers who had remained faithful to Vichy, he was to be dismissed from the service. But since a senior officer who had known him when he was a young second lieutenant at Chi-Ma intervened in his behalf, Captain Trinquier was assigned, on February 1, 1947, to Tarbes and Pau, where the French airborne training center had been created. (The officer who had saved Trinquier's career was himself an old "Indochina hand," General Raoul Salan, later commander-inchief in Indochina and Algeria. In 1961 he was to lead the revolt against General de Gaulle's Algerian policies; caught and convicted of attempting to overthrow the French Republic, Salan is now serving a life sentence in a French military prison.)

On November 14, 1947, Trinquier again landed in Indochina as second-in-command of the Ist Colonial Parachute Battalion, whose command he was to assume in September, 1948, after its commander had been killed in action. Promoted to the rank of major, Trinquier and his unit participated in the grim inch-by-inch clearing operations on the Plain of Reeds—he was to parachute into it four times—and in southern Central Vietnam. Those are exactly the same areas in which Vietnamese troops and their American advisers are heavily involved today.

After another tour of duty in France as commander of the Commando Training Center in Fréjus and of the Colonial Paratroop School, Trinquier returned to Indochina in December, 1951, to take over a brand-new service just created by Marshal Jean de Lattre de Tassigny, France's best commander-in-chief in the Far East. (Regrettably, he was to die of cancer within a year.) De Lattre had decided to turn the Vietminh's skill in fighting behind the lines against the Vietminh itself by implanting anti-Communist guerrillas deep inside the enemy's territory, In view of his knowledge of the northern hill areas and tribal groups, Trinquier was selected as the leader for the northern operations; his first efforts were soon crowned with success, for contact team after contact team was dropped into enemy territory, and, contrary to expectations, most managed to survive and fight.

When Trinquier's methods became known to the American military advisers in Saigon, he was invited to visit American antiguerrilla-training centers in Korea and Japan. Two young American officers also returned with him to Indochina to learn from his operations, and American equipment for his guerrilla units became readily available. By mid-1951, Major Trinquier received command of all behind-the-lines operations in Indochina, and his units became officially known as GCMA, or Groupements de Commandos Mixtes Aéroportés (Composite Airborne Commando Groups), a name that was changed, in December, 1953, to GMI (Groupement Mixte d'Intervention, or Composite Intervention Group), when their mission was extended beyond airborne commando operations.

By late 1953, almost 20,000 men were under his command—probably the largest unit ever commanded by an army major—and engaged in operations covering several thousand square miles of enemy territory. Native tribesmen were flocking to his maquis in greater numbers than could be armed and trained; but before he could make full use of them, what Trinquier—in a masterly understatement—calls "the regrettable Dien Bien Phu incident" ended the Indochina war. What followed was a horrible debacle: Thousands of partisans had to be abandoned to the enemy, since the stipulations of the Geneva cease-fire of 1954 did not permit the French to continue to supply them.

Trinquier asserts that he had asked the United States, which had not signed the cease-fire agreement, to continue to supply the guerrillas, but that his request had been turned down. Although the partisans and their French cadres fought on long beyond the cease-fire, they were eventually wiped out one by one.[2] In his final operations report (which I found in some forgotten archives in Paris), Trinquier could not help but show some of his deep feelings about his abandoned men:

> The total suppression of logistical support . . . will bring in its wake the progressive liquidation of our [infiltrated] elements. There is little hope of seeing the leaders of our maquis escape the "clemency" of President Ho Chi Minh.
>
> As of August 15, 1954, fifteen enemy regular battalions, fifteen regional battalions and seventeen regional companies are now committed against them. Ceasing operations as per orders at the very moment when they were about to

triumph, our maquis, undefeated on the field of battle, have been offered up for sacrifice.

While the [GCMA] command has, with discipline, accepted the sacrifice of the maquis, it no longer feels morally authorized to ask its partisans to remain at our disposal.

In this bloodthirsty adventure, their only consolation remains the pride of having won the last successes of that campaign, and of having created a veritable popular uprising against the Vietminh.

During those decisive years in Indochina, Trinquier began to study in depth the principles of "modern warfare," of which the pages that follow will give a detailed account, but the years of combat in Algeria that were to follow probably added a political dimension that was heretofore lacking in him. Assigned as a lieutenant-colonel to the 10th Parachute Division of General Massu (another old Indochina hand), he narrowly missed the Suez invasion of 1956—another perfect illustration, from his point of view, of the frustration by politics of what seemed to be a "sound" military operation—and found himself assigned, with all the other units of the 10th, to clearing the town of Algiers of all terrorists. Bomb- and grenade-throwing in Algiers had, in 1957, become an everyday occurrence, against which the regular police was all but powerless.

Massu, Trinquier, and the camouflage-clad paratroopers of the 10th "waded" into the situation with a cold ferocity that made headlines throughout the world and provided Lartéguy's *The Centurions* with its choicest passages. It also provided Trinquier with a Cartesian rationale for the use of torture in revolutionary war; torture is the particular bane of the terrorist, just as antiaircraft artillery is that of the airman or machinegun fire that of the foot soldier. Trinquier's methods won the day in Algiers; but the dying Fourth Republic felt that it could not afford to let him remain much longer in the public eye, and Trinquier temporarily went to command the French Airborne Center at Pau.

But his old protector, General Salan, soon recalled him to Algeria to become the commander of the 3d Colonial Airborne Regiment. That unit took on the onerous task of sealing off the Tunisian border south of the "Morice Line"—the electronic 300-kilometer-long fence constructed by the French Army from the Mediterranean to the desert—along its Saharan fringe. As Trinquier was to describe in detail in another book,[3] he found himself by accident rather than design in the Algiers area when the May 13, 1958, putsch in Algiers led to the return of General de Gaulle to power, but he nevertheless took an important part in establishing the famous Public Safety Committee of Algiers.

Soon in disagreement with de Gaulle's policies, he returned to the command of his regiment to participate in the mop-up operations of the "Challe

Plan," named after the new commander-in-chief, Air Force General Challe. Between July, 1959, and March, 1960, the 3d Airborne, in a series of relentless pursuits, broke the Algerian nationalists' hold on one of the most difficult areas in Algeria, El Milia. Militarily, the end seemed in sight, but, internationally, pressures had begun to build up against France. The Algerian war was expensive, all the newly independent nations were turning against France, and even her own allies no longer voted with her in the United Nations. In a history-making "tour of the officers' messes" (*"la tournée des popotes"*) in March, 1960, de Gaulle explained to his officers in Algeria that, inevitably, the country would achieve independence.

To the new generation of technicians of revolutionary warfare, that political solution was abhorrent. Not swayed by the international implications of the situation, they believed that to abandon Algeria when military victory seemed so near for the first time would be not only another rank betrayal of a personal commitment but also a direct condemnation of their methods of combat. The reaction that set in was to lead many of them out of the army and into prison—and a few to the firing squad.

Trinquier himself was, beyond a doubt, saved by circumstances. While the Algerian storm was brewing, he had been recalled from his command to help President Moise Tshombe of Katanga Province organize his white-cadred forces. He had arrived in Elisabethville on January 25, 1961; he was expelled from Katanga on March 9, under Belgian and U.N. pressure. He was in Athens writing up his recommendations for Katanga when most of his former associates became involved, on April 21, 1961, in the abortive "generals' mutiny" in Algiers. His army career, at best, was finished, and his request to be put on the retired list met with no opposition.

But Trinquier seems to have found a new avocation in political writing and lecturing, which may indicate that he has certain political ambitions for the future. It would be difficult to classify him by American standards as *radically* "right wing," for his acquaintance with Mao leads him to accept the need for social reforms as an instrument in defeating Communism. In his recent writings, however, he has attacked what he considers to be the high-handed methods of the Fifth Republic in the field of civil liberties; yet his own writings clearly show that he would not shrink from using the same methods, if necessary, himself.

To be sure, the informed reader will find in the following pages much that will shock him or that will strike him as incredible. In many cases, Trinquier, like any other person who is certain he holds the key to absolute truth, underplays the difficulties some of his counterinsurgency measures are likely to raise and encounter or neglects to explain all the failures satisfactorily. For example, although it is true that the GCMA's tied down a Vietminh force three times their own size during the battle of Dien Bien Phu, they never succeeded in seriously hampering Communist supply lines to the besieged fortress. Likewise, there has never been solid evidence to prove that a real effort was made—as Trinquier advocates here—to infiltrate counterguerrilla maquis into Tunisia to attack Algerian bases; or that such maquis, if they ever existed, were successful.

But on the other hand, American readers—particularly those who are concerned with today's operations in South Vietnam—will find to their surprise that their various seemingly "new" counterinsurgency gambits, from strategic hamlets to large-scale pacification, are mere rehashes of old tactics to which helicopters, weed killers, and rapid-firing rifles merely add a new dimension of speed and bloodiness without basically changing the character of the struggle—nor its outcome, if the same *political* errors that the French have made are repeated. And the careers of Trinquier and of his numerous comrades still in the French Army prove that France has an ample reserve of counterinsurgency specialists whose qualifications are second to none.

It is, once again, Larténguy who brings into sharp focus that type of soldier, when one of his key characters, just such a revolutionary-warfare colonel, jokingly states that France should have two armies—one with "lovely guns" and "distinguished and doddering generals," and the other "composed entirely of young enthusiasts in camouflaged battle dress, who would not be put on display, but from whom impossible efforts would be demanded. . . ." To which another character answers with a warning: "You're heading for a lot of trouble."

But the trouble into which a regular army must inevitably—perhaps fatally—run when it is committed to a long string of revolutionary wars is only dimly perceived in America so far. Colonel Trinquier's book should do much to serve as a timely warning.

Bernard B. Fall
Alexandria, Virginia
October, 1963

NOTES

1. Jean Larténguy, *The Centurions* (New York: E. P. Dutton & Co., 1961; New York: Avon Book Corp., 1962 [paperback]).

2. For a more detailed description of GCMA operations, see Bernard Fall, *Street Without Joy: Indochina at War, 1946-1963* (3d rev. ed.; Harrisburg: Stackpole, 1963).

3. Roger Trinquier, *Le coup d'etat du 13 mai* (Paris: Editions l'Esprit Nouveau, 1963).

Part One

PREPARATION FOR WAR

Chapter 1

THE NEED TO ADAPT OUR MILITARY APPARATUS TO MODERN WARFARE

The defense of national territory is the *raison d'être* of an army; it should always be capable of accomplishing this objective.

Since the liberation of France in 1945, however, the French Army has not been able to halt the collapse of our Empire. And yet, the effort the country has made for the army is unprecedented. No French military man ought to rest until we have created an army at last capable of assuring the defense of our national territory.

We still persist in studying a type of warfare that no longer exists and that we shall never fight again, while we pay only passing attention to the war we lost in Indochina and the one we are about to lose in Algeria. Yet the abandonment of Indochina or of Algeria is just as important for France as would be the loss of a metropolitan province.

The result of this shortcoming is that the army is not prepared to confront an adversary employing arms and methods the army itself ignores. It has, therefore, no chance of winning.

It is a fact that in Indochina, despite a marked superiority in materiel and in troops, we were beaten. From one campaign to another, our commanders tried to drive the Vietminh into a classic pitched battle, the only kind we knew how to fight, in hope that our superiority in materiel would allow an easy victory. The Vietminh always knew how to elude such maneuvers. When they finally accepted the conventional battle so vainly sought for several years, it was only because they had assembled on the battlefield resources superior to our own. That was at Dien Bien Phu in May, 1954.

Despite the record, our army is employing, with few exceptions, the identical combat procedures in North Africa. We are trying in the course of repeated complex operations to seize an adversary who eludes us. The results obtained bear no relation to the resources and efforts expended. In fact, we are only dispersing, rather than destroying, the attacked bands.

Our military machine reminds one of a pile driver attempting to crush a fly, indefatigably persisting in repeating its efforts.

The inability of the army to adapt itself to changed circurnstances has heavy consequences. It gives credence to the belief that our adversaries, who represent only weak forces, are invincible and that, sooner or later, we shall have to accept their conditions for peace. It encourages the diffusion of dangerously erroneous ideas, which eventually become generally accepted. France is accused of having conducted rigged elections in Algeria, and one is led to believe that those carried out under the aegis of the (Algerian) National Liberation Front (F.L.N.) would be genuine. At the same time, it is well known that any threat that would subsequently confront the voters would be effective in quite a different way from the former, merely administrative, pressures.

All this is nonetheless what a large part of our own press tries to tell the public.

We know that it is not at all necessary to have the sympathy of a majority of the people in order to rule them. The right organization can turn the trick.

This is what our adversaries are accomplishing in Algeria. Thanks to a *specially adapted organization* and to appropriate methods of warfare, they have been successful in imposing themselves upon entire populations and in using them, despite their own desires in the matter, against us. Our enemies are submitting us to a kind of hateful extortion, to which we shall have to accede in the end if we cannot destroy the warfare system that confronts us. We would be gravely remiss in our duty if we should permit ourselves to be thus deluded and to abandon the struggle before final victory. We would be sacrificing defenseless populations to unscrupulous enemies.

Chapter 2

MODERN WARFARE DEFINED

Since the end of World War II, a new form of warfare has been born. Called at times either *subversive warfare* or *revolutionary warfare,* it differs fundamentally from the wars of the past in that victory is not expected from the clash of two armies on a field of battle. This confrontation, which in times past saw the annihilation of an enemy army in one or more battles, no longer occurs.

Warfare is now an interlocking system of actions—political, economic, psychological, military—that aims at the *overthrow of the established authority in a country and its replacement by another regime.* To achieve this end, the aggressor tries to exploit the internal tensions of the country attacked—ideological, social, religious, economic—any conflict liable to have a profound influence on the population to be conquered. Moreover, in view of the present-day interdependence of nations, any residual grievance within a population, no matter how localized and lacking in scope, will surely be brought by determined adversaries into the framework of the great world conflict. From a localized conflict of secondary origin and importance, they will always attempt sooner or later to bring about a generalized conflict.

On so vast a field of action, traditional armed forces no longer enjoy their accustomed decisive role. Victory no longer depends on one battle over a given terrain. Military operations, as combat actions carried out against opposing armed forces, are of only limited importance and are never the total conflict.

This is doubtless the reason why the army, traditionally attracted by the purely military aspect of a conflict, has never seriously approached the study of a problem it considers an inferior element in the art of war.

A modern army is first of all one that is capable of winning the conflict in which its country is engaged. And we are certainly at war, because we run the risk of being finally defeated on the ground (as at Dien Bien Phu in May, 1954) and because, in case of such a defeat, we shall have to cede vast territories to our opponents.

The struggle we have been carrying on for fifteen years, in Indochina as well as in Algeria, is truly a war. But what we are involved in is *modern warfare.*

If we want to win, it is in this light that we must consider it from now on.

Studies have been made in many countries of what is called subversive warfare. But they rarely go beyond the stage of guerrilla warfare, which comes closest to the traditional form.

Mindful of the Allied victory in World War II, and perhaps because it is more appealing to study successful combat methods than to dwell upon the reasons for a defeat, only the offensive use of the guerrilla has been considered. But the study of effective countermeasures has been neglected. Some authors have stressed the inadequacy of the means employed against the guerrilla; others have simply counseled reacting against the guerrilla—confronting him with the counterguerrilla to beat him at his own game.

This is to wish to resolve a problem quickly without having duly weighed it.

The subtlest aspects of *modern warfare,* such as the manipulation of populations, have been the subject of recent studies. But only some of the methods employed by an enemy to consolidate his hold over conquered populations in peacetime have been investigated, in particular the working of psychological action on the masses.

But the rallying of opposition and the study of effective means of protection have been neglected. More exactly, when the enemy's methods and their application have been recognized, propaganda and pressures have always been powerful enough to influence a poorly informed public and to lead it systematically to refuse to study or use the same methods.

We know that the *sine qua non* of victory in *modern warfare* is the unconditional support of a population. According to Mao Tse-tung, it is as essential to the combatant as water to the fish. Such support may be spontaneous, although that is quite rare and probably a temporary condition. If it doesn't exist, it must be secured by every possible means, the most effective of which is *terrorism.*

In *modern warfare*, we are not actually grappling with an army organized along traditional lines, but with a few armed elements acting clandestinely within a population manipulated by a special organization.

Our army in Algeria is in excess of 300,000 men supplied with the most modern equipment; its adversary numbers some 30,000, in general poorly equipped with only light weapons.

If we were to have an opportunity to meet this enemy on the traditional field of battle, a dream vainly pursued for years by many military commanders, victory would be assured in a matter of hours.

The war has lasted more than six years, however, and victory is still uncertain. The problem is more complex.

In seeking a solution, it is essential to realize that in *modern warfare* we are not up against just a few armed bands spread across a given territory, but rather against an *armed clandestine organization* whose essential role is to impose its will upon the population. Victory will be obtained only through the complete destruction of that organization. This is the master concept that must guide us in our study of *modern warfare*.

Chapter 3

AN EXAMPLE OF A CLANDESTINE WARFARE ORGANIZATION

One example of a clandestine warfare organization is that operating in the city of Algiers during 1956–57. It was constituted as an autonomous zone by the National Liberation Front (F.L.N.), but was related to the F.L.N. setup throughout Algeria.

The Autonomous Zone of Algiers (Z.A.A.) operated under a council of four members: a political-military leader, a political assistant, a military assistant, and an assistant for external liaison and intelligence. Decisions were made in common, but the vote of the political-military leader counted heaviest.

The city and its suburbs were divided into three regions—Central Algiers, Algiers West, and Algiers East—which operated under regional councils identical to the zonal council. Each region was divided into sectors, which, in turn, were subdivided into districts. In all, the Z.A.A.'s three regions comprised ten sectors, or thirty-four districts.

The organization of the Z.A.A. contained two distinct elements: the National Liberation Front (F.L.N.), or political arm, and the National Liberation Army (A.L.N.), or military arm. Both were integrated into the same geographical breakdown, but were highly compartmented and were united only at the regional and zonal levels.

Units of the A.L.N. and F.L.N. worked side by side in each district, but the regional council was responsible for coordination of their action.

The political organization (F.L.N.) of each district—based on the demi-cell of three men, then the cell, the demi-group, the group, and the sub-district—was under the command of a district leader, who controlled 127 men (see the table below).

The military organization (A.L.N.) of the district consisted of 35 armed men. The district commander and his deputy were at the head of three armed groups, each headed by a leader and deputy and composed of three cells of three men each.

(The political organization had at its disposal some armed shock groups of its own that were not part of the A.L.N.; they constituted the F.L.N.'s "police" and were charged with the execution of sentences pronounced by their judiciary.)

The zonal council assistant for external liaison and intelligence had at his disposal a certain number of committees in which were grouped the F.L.N.'s intellectuals. The following were the principal committees and their duties.

Demi-Cell	Cell	Demi-Group	Group	Sub-District	District
1 Demi-Cell	2 Demi-Cells plus a Cell Leader	2 Cells plus a Demi-Group Leader	2 Demi-Groups plus a Group Leader	2 Groups plus a Sub-District Leader	2 Sub-Districts plus a District Leader
3 men	7 men	15 men	31 men	63 men	127 men

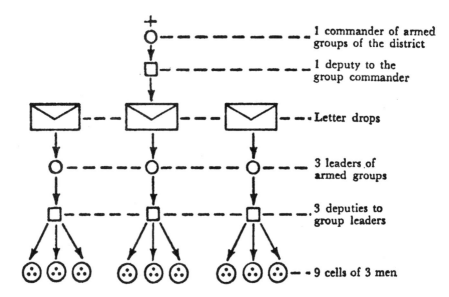

1 commander of armed groups of the district

1 deputy to the group commander

Letter drops

3 leaders of armed groups

3 deputies to group leaders

9 cells of 3 men

- Liaison Committee—maintained contact with the *wilayas,* or major military districts (Algeria was divided by the F.L.N. into six *wilayas*); with the Committee for External Coordination (C.C.E.), forerunner of the present Provisional Government of the Algerian Republic (G.P.R.A.); and with the Exterior: Tunisia, Morocco, France.
- Information Committee—at that time the embryo of the special services.
- Editorial Committee—maintained United Nations dossiers, "reprisal" dossiers, relations with the intellectuals, documentation for the French and other foreign press, etc.
- Justice Committee—general surveillance of French citizens of Moslem origin (F.M.A.); judged cases between Moslems in civil and criminal law, imposed various fines, etc.
- Financial Committee—gathered funds from the population at large, using units of the F.L.N., and, in larger amounts, directly from big companies, banks, leading merchants, etc.
- Health Committee—embryonic in Algiers. The sick and wounded were mostly cared for in secret in the hospitals of the city.
- Trade Union Committee—maintained permanent contact with various syndical organizations, such as the General Union of Algerian Workers (U.G.T.A.) and the General Union of Algerian Merchants (U.G.C.A.).

A final important element of the whole Z.A.A. organization was the bomb-throwing network directly responsible to the zonal council. Carefully kept apart from other elements of the organization, the network was broken down into a number of quite distinct and compartmented branches, in communication only with the network chief through a system of letter boxes.

A chart of the organization of the bomb-throwing network is shown below.

In the city of Algiers alone, the clandestine warfare organization comprised approximately 1,200 armed men (A.L.N.), and 4,500 persons unarmed or semiarmed (F.L.N.). At that time, there were scarcely a thousand police, equipped only to fight common criminals in time of peace. Taken by surprise by an adversary of which it was totally ignorant, the police had no chance of coming out on top. The army's intervention was therefore unavoidable.

A clandestine organization of such size and complexity requires for its creation both time and a precise technique.

The higher cadres, up to regional level, had all received a more or less thorough Marxist training; they had entered the organization voluntarily.

The lower cadres and the rank-and-file were at first recruited from the seamier elements of the city, delinquents or habitual criminals. By the very

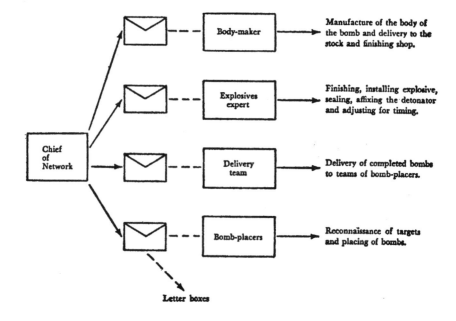

fact of their pasts, they were already quite well adapted to the missions they were going to be assigned.

Later on, the organization received a constant influx of new members which kept up or augmented its forces. The manner in which they were recruited has been revealed to us through numerous interrogations. To the question "How did you enter the A.L.N.?"—which was often put to them—most of the young terrorists replied:

"I was a good worker and was earning an honest living, One day, I was stopped by a fellow who insisted I pay a certain sum to the F.L.N. At first I refused, and was beaten up by the three men he had with him. I paid. The next month the same sum was asked. I paid it without argument. Some time later, I became a collector myself. I received a list of persons who were to contribute and a small armed team to protect me during the collection. Then, as I was athletic and in good health, I was asked to enter into the armed organization—the A.L.N.—the Army of National Liberation. I wanted to refuse, but a few pointed threats made me accept. From that time on I was lost, because to be admitted to the A.L.N., one first had to prove his worth; that is, to carry out an armed attack in the city. The conditions under which this was to be accomplished were explained to me. One evening, at a fixed time and an appointed place, an individual unknown to me was to give me a loaded weapon with the mission to kill the first person I came across. I was then to flee, dropping the weapon into a trashcan that the unknown person had pointed out to me. I did what was required of me and, three days later, I entered as a member into a cell of the A.L.N."

It was in this manner in the month of January, 1957, that Doctor X of Algiers was assassinated by a young man who did not even know the name of his victim.

The means of putting pressure on the citizenry were quite varied. The following is an example of one used by the members of the zonal council to assure their own security:

When one or several members of the council wanted to install themselves in a house in the Casbah, they first sent a team of masons to construct a hiding place there. The masons immediately gathered together the people in the building and told them, in substance: "You are soon to receive important personages. You will be responsible for their security with your lives." And sometimes, to indicate that this was no idle threat, a burst of gunfire cut down on the spot the residents who seemed to them most suspect. From then on, the movements of the residents were strictly controlled; never could more than half of them be outside at a time. The secret was well kept.

Yassef Saadi, political-military commissar of the Z.A.A. was able to install himself within 200 yards of the office of the army commandant of the Algiers sector and remain there without being found for several months before his arrest.

Chapter 4

TERRORISM—THE PRINCIPAL WEAPON OF MODERN WARFARE

The war in Indochina and the one in Algeria have demonstrated the basic weapon that permits our enemies to fight effectively with few resources and even to defeat a traditional army.

This weapon is *terrorism.*

Terrorism in the service of a clandestine organization devoted to manipulating the population is a recent development. After being used in Morocco in 1954, it reached its full development in Algiers in December, 1956, and January, 1957. The resultant surprise gave our adversaries an essential advantage, which may have been decisive. In effect, a hundred organized terrorists were all that was necessary to cause us to give up the game quickly to the Moroccans.

Terrorism, then, is a *weapon of warfare,* which can neither be ignored nor minimized. It is as a weapon of warfare that we should study it.

The goal of *modern warfare* is control of the populace, and terrorism is a particularly appropriate weapon, since it aims directly at the inhabitant. In the street, at work, at home, the citizen lives continually under the threat of violent death. In the presence of this permanent danger surrounding him, he has the depressing feeling of being an isolated and defenseless target. The fact that public authority and the police are no longer capable of ensuring his security adds to his distress. He loses confidence in the state whose inherent mission it is to guarantee his safety. He is more and more drawn to the side of the terrorists, who alone are able to protect him.

The intended objective, which is to cause the population to vacillate is thus attained.

What characterizes modern terrorism, and makes for its basic strength, is the slaughter of generally defenseless persons. The terrorist operates within a familiar legal framework, while avoiding the ordinary risks taken by the common criminal, let alone by soldiers on the field of battle, or even by partisans facing regular troops.

The ordinary criminal kills a certain individual, usually only one, for a specific purpose. Having achieved it, he may no longer constitute a danger to society. His crime is based on an easily discernible motive—robbery, vengeance, etc. To succeed, he quite often has to run risks sufficient to cause his arrest. His crime is thus carried out within a known framework. Well-defined police procedure can easily be applied, which takes whatever time is necessary to obtain justice, while respecting the rights of both the individual and society.

The soldier meets his adversary on the field of battle and in uniform. He fights within a framework of traditional rules that both sides respect. Aware of the dangers that confront him, the soldier has always had a high regard for his opponent, because both run the same risks. When the battle is over, the dead and the wounded of the two camps are treated with the same humanity; prisoners are withdrawn as quickly as possible from the battlefield and are simply kept from fighting again until the end of the war.

For the partisan and the irregular who oppose a regular army, the very fact that they violate the rules of warfare in fighting without a uniform (avoiding the risks involved) deprives them of the protection of these same rules. If taken prisoner while armed, they may be shot on the spot.

But the case of the terrorist is quite otherwise. Not only does he carry on warfare without uniform, but he attacks, far from a field of battle, only unarmed civilians who are incapable of defending themselves and who are normally protected under the rules of warfare. Surrounded by a vast organization, which prepares his task and assists him in its execution, which assures his withdrawal and his protection, he runs practically no risks— neither that of retaliation by his victims nor that of having to appear before a court of justice. When it has been decided to kill someone sometime somewhere, with the sole purpose of terrorizing the populace and strewing a certain number of bodies along the streets of a city or on country roads, it is quite easy under existing laws to escape the police.

In Algiers, during 1956, the F.L.N. set up the clandestine warfare organization already described, and it was impossible for the police forces to arrest a single terrorist. In the face of the ever increasing number of attacks, the police ought to have acknowledged their impotence and appealed to the army.

Without the massive intervention of the army (in particular of the Tenth Parachute Division) at the beginning of 1957, the entire city would have fallen into the hands of the F.L.N., the loss carrying with it the immediate abandonment of all Algeria.

In a large city, police forces can partly restrict the action of the terrorists and delay their complete control of the populace. Obliged to act secretly, the organization's functioning will be slow and difficult. Massive and drastic action by the army may even be able to stop it entirely, as in Algiers in 1957.

But in the unprotected regions that comprise the major portion of the national territory, particularly the vast area of inhabited countryside where police forces are small or nonexistent, terrorist action encounters no opposition at the beginning of a conflict and is most effective.

Isolated raids first reveal the existence of a partially organized movement. These attract attention and promote caution among the populace. Then, selective terrorism begins to eliminate lesser persons of influence, petty bureaucrats and various police officials who did not understand the first warnings or were slow in reacting to them. Administrative cadres are restrained or eliminated. The silence and collusion of the unprotected inhabitants have been won. Agents of the enemy have a free hand to organize and to manipulate the population at will.

From then on, within the midst of these people taken over by terrorism, the small armed bands whose task it is to wage guerrilla warfare are able to install themselves, in the phrase of Mao Tse-tung, like fish in water. Fed, informed, protected, they are able to strike without difficulty against the forces of order.

Modern warfare requires the unconditional support of the populace. This support must be maintained at any price. Here again, terrorism plays its role.

An unceasing watch is exercised over all the inhabitants. Any suspicion or indication of lack of submission is punishable by death, quite often preceded by horrible torture.

The atrocities committed by the F.L.N. in Algeria to maintain its hold over the populace are innumerable. I will cite but one example to demonstrate the degree to which they were carried in certain areas.

In the month of September, 1958, the forces of order took possession of the files of a military tribunal of one of the regions of the F.L.N. In the canton of Michelet alone, in the arrondissement (district) of Fort-National in Kabylie, more than 2,000 inhabitants were condemned to death and executed between November 1, 1954, and April 17, 1957.

Quite clearly, terrorism is a weapon of warfare, and it is important to stress it.

Although quite old, until recently it has been utilized only by isolated revolutionaries for spectacular attacks, principally against high political personalities, such as sovereigns, chiefs of state, and ministers. Even in Indochina, where guerrillas achieved such a remarkable degree of development that it permitted the Vietminh finally to win, terrorism has never been systematically employed. For example, the plastic bomb attacks outside the municipal theater in Saigon, which caused the greatest number of victims, were not carried out by the Vietminh (see Graham Greene's book *The Quiet American*).

The terrorist should not be considered an ordinary criminal. Actually, he fights within the framework of his organization, without personal interest, for a cause he considers noble and for a respectable ideal, the same as the soldiers in the armies confronting him. On the command of his superiors, he kills without hatred individuals unknown to him, with the same indifference as the soldier on the battlefield. His victims are often women and children, almost always defenseless individuals taken by surprise. But during a period of history when the bombing of open cities is permitted, and when two Japanese cities were razed to hasten the end of the war in the Pacific, one cannot with good cause reproach him.[1]

The terrorist has become a soldier, like the aviator or the infantryman.

But the aviator flying over a city knows that antiaircraft shells can kill or maim him. The infantryman wounded on the battlefield accepts physical suffering, often for long hours, when he falls between the lines and it is impossible to rescue him. It never occurs to him to complain and to ask, for example, that his enemy renounce the use of the rifle, the shell, or the bomb. If he can, he goes back to a hospital knowing this to be his lot. The soldier, therefore, admits the possibility of physical suffering as part of the job. The risks he runs on the battlefield and the suffering he endures are the price of the glory he receives.

The terrorist claims the same honors while rejecting the same obligations. His kind of organization permits him to escape from the police, his victims cannot defend themselves, and the army cannot use the power of its weapons against him because he hides himself permanently within the midst of a population going about its peaceful pursuits.

But he must be made to realize that, when he is captured, he cannot be treated as an ordinary criminal, nor like a prisoner taken on the battlefield. What the forces of order who have arrested him are seeking is not to punish a crime, for which he is otherwise not personally responsible, but, as in any war, the destruction of the enemy army or its surrender. Therefore he is not asked details about himself or about attacks that he may or may not have committed and that are not of immediate interest, but rather for precise information about his organization. In particular, each man has a superior whom he knows; he will first have to give the name of this person, along with his address, so that it will be possible to proceed with the arrest without delay.

No lawyer is present for such an interrogation. If the prisoner gives the information requested, the examination is quickly terminated; if not, specialists must force his secret from him. Then, as a soldier, he must face the suffering, and perhaps the death, he has heretofore managed to avoid. The terrorist must accept this as a condition inherent in his trade and in the methods of warfare that, with full knowledge, his superiors and he himself have chosen.[2] Once the interrogation is finished, however, the terrorist can take his place among soldiers. From then on, he is a prisoner of war like any other, kept from resuming hostilities until the end of the conflict.

It would be as useless and unjust to charge him with the attacks he was able to carry out, as to hold responsible the infantryman or the airman for the deaths caused by the weapons they use. According to Clausewitz:

> War . . . is an act of violence intended to compel an opponent to fulfill our will. . . . Self-imposed restrictions, almost imperceptible and hardly worth mentioning, termed usages of International Law, accompany it without impairing its power. Violence . . . is therefore the means; the compulsory submission of the enemy to our will is the ultimate object. . . . In such dangerous things as war, the errors which proceed from a spirit of benevolence are the worst. As the use of physical power to the utmost extent by no means excludes the cooperation of the intelligence, it follows that he who uses force unsparingly, without reference to the bloodshed involved, must obtain a superiority if his adversary uses less vigor in its application. . . .
>
> To introduce into the philosophy of war itself a principle of moderation would be an absurdity.[3]

These basic principles of traditional warfare retain all of their validity in *modern warfare*.

Although violence is an unavoidable necessity in warfare, certain unnecessary violence ought to be rigorously banned. Interrogations in *modern warfare* should be conducted by specialists perfectly versed in the techniques to be employed.

The first condition for a quick and effective interrogation is to have interrogators who know what they can ask the terrorist under questioning. For this, it is first of all essential to place him precisely within the diagram of the organization to which he belongs. A profound knowledge of the organization is required. It is useless to ask a funds collector about caches of weapons or bombs. Every clandestine organization is strictly compartmented, and he would know nothing about them. To ask him would be a useless waste of time. On the other hand, he does know to whom he remits the funds and under what conditions. This is the only subject about which he should be questioned.

It is known that the ordinary terrorist operates as part of a three-man team; therefore he knows his comrade and his demi-cell superior. This is the only information he will be able to furnish, but he must give it quickly; otherwise, the individuals sought will have the time to disappear, the thread will be broken, and a lengthy search will quite often come to naught.

The interrogators must always strive not to injure the physical and moral integrity of individuals. Science can easily place at the army's disposition the means for obtaining what is sought.

But we must not trifle with our responsibilities. It is deceitful to permit artillery or aviation to bomb villages and slaughter women and children, while the real enemy usually escapes, and to refuse interrogation specialists the right to seize the truly guilty terrorist and spare the innocent.

Terrorism in the hands of our adversaries has become a formidable weapon of war that we can no longer permit ourselves to ignore. Tried out in Indochina and brought to perfection in Algeria, it can lead to any boldness, even a direct attack on metropolitan France. Thanks to the Communist Party, which is already on the scene and is familiar with underground operations, it would encounter no great difficulty.

Even a band of gangsters, lacking any political ideology at all, but without scruples and determined to employ the same methods, could constitute a grave danger.

In the light of present events, we can imagine in its broad outlines the unfolding of future aggression:

A few organized and well-trained men of action will carry out a reign of terror in the big cities. If the goal pursued is only to strew the streets nightly with a certain number of anonymous corpses to terrorize the inhabitants, a specialized organization would have no difficulty, within the framework of existing laws, in escaping the pursuit of the police. The numerous attacks being committed nightly in our large cities, which are nothing other than a prelude to facilitating the creation and training of an important warfare organization, demonstrate in a tangible way the inadequacy of a traditional police force against modern terrorists. Whenever a broad attack is unfolded, the police run the risk of being quickly overwhelmed.

In the countryside, and particularly in the hilly regions such as the Massif Central, the Alps, or Brittany, the population has no permanent protection. Small bands could easily block traffic through difficult passes by killing the passengers of the first two or three automobiles. A few brutalities, such as savagely executed preventive assassinations in the surrounding villages, will cow the inhabitants into providing for the maintenance of the bands and will discourage them from giving useful information to the authorities.

Occasional police operations timidly carried out with inadequate forces will fail pitifully. These failures will encourage a goodly number of adventurers to team up with the original outlaws, who will rapidly develop into rebels.

In this fashion, immense zones will be practically abandoned to our adversaries and will be lost to our control. The way will be open to the guerrilla. With terrorism in the cities and guerrillas in the countryside, the war will have begun. This is the simple mechanism, now well known, which can at any instant be unleashed against us.

NOTES

1. Yassef Saadi, chief of the Autonomous Zone of Algiers (Z.A.A.), said after his arrest: "I had my bombs planted in the city because I didn't have the aircraft to transport them. But they caused fewer victims than the artillery and air bombardments of our mountain villages. I'm in a war, you cannot blame me."

2. In France during the Nazi occupation, members of the Resistance violated the rules of warfare. They knew they could not hide behind them, and they were perfectly aware of the risks to which they were exposing themselves. Their glory is to have calmly faced those risks with full knowledge of the consequences.

3. Karl von Clausewitz, *On War*, trans. Col. J. J. Graham (New York: E. P. Dutton and Co.), 1, 2–3.

Chapter 5

IDENTIFYING THE ADVERSARY

To carry out a war effectively, to win it, it is indispensable to identify the adversary exactly. This condition must be fulfilled so that our shots will strike home.

Formerly, this was a simple task. According to the period of our history, he was to be found on the other side of the Rhine or the other side of the Channel. He had his war aims, simple and precise, as we had ours. It would have been useless to attempt to convert him to our cause or to hope to cause him to give up the fight without having defeated him.

To gain a victory, the nation and its army put to work all material and moral resources. Any person who dealt with the enemy, or who favored his objectives in any way, was considered a traitor and was treated as such.

In *modern warfare,* the enemy is far more difficult to identify. No physical frontier separates the two camps. The line of demarcation between friend and foe passes through the very heart of the nation, through the same village, and sometimes divides the same family. It is a non-physical, often ideological boundary, which must however be expressly delineated if we want to reach the adversary and to defeat him.

Since *the military art is simply and completely one of action,* it is only when we have identified the enemy that the apparently complex problems posed to the army by *modern warfare* can be reduced to realistic proportions and easily resolved. The criteria for arriving at such a point will be difficult to establish; however, a study of the causes of the war and the aims pursued by the adversary will permit us to discover them.

The period of preparation before the opening of hostilities generally takes place under cover of a legally established political party; our opponents can thus get themselves within our frontiers and under the protection of our laws. Covered by legality, they will strive to create a climate favorable to their cause within the country and abroad and to establish on our own territory the essential elements of their warfare organization.

The fact that *modern warfare* is not officially declared, that a state of war is not generally proclaimed, permits the adversary to continue to take advantage of peacetime legislation, to pursue his activities both openly and secretly. He will strive by every means to preserve the fiction of peace, which is so essential to the pursuit of his design.

Therefore, the surest means of unveiling the adversary is to declare a state of war at the earliest moment, at the very latest when the first symptoms of the struggle are revealed in political assassinations, terrorism, guerrilla activities, etc.

At this stage the preparation of the opponent will be quite well advanced and the danger very great; to minimize this would be a disastrous mistake. Henceforth, any party that has supported or continues to support the enemy shall be considered a party of the enemy.

The nation attacked must fall in behind the government and its army. An army can throw itself into a campaign only when it has the moral support of the nation; it is the nation's faithful reflection because it is composed of the nation's youth and because it carries within it the hopes of the nation. Its unquestioned actions should be praised by the nation to maintain the nobility of the just cause it has been charged to make triumphant. The army, whose responsibility it is to do battle, must receive the unreserved, affectionate, and devoted support of the nation. Any propaganda tending to undermine its morale, causing it to doubt the necessity of its sacrifices, should be unmercifully repressed.

The army will then know where to strike. Any individual who, in any fashion whatsoever, favors the objectives of the enemy will be considered a traitor and treated as such.

In totalitarian countries, ideological boundaries are extended to the country's geographic limits, so that there may be no doubt as to the enemy to be struck. All enemies of the established power are eliminated or driven out of the national territory.

Although we should avoid these extreme measures, which are unquestionably incompatible with the ideals of liberty dear to us and to the civilization we are defending, we cannot, obviously, defeat an enemy we have not clearly identified.

We know that the *enemy* consists not of a few armed bands fighting on the ground, but of an organization that feeds him, informs him, and sustains his morale. This is a state of affairs that democracy tolerates within an attacked nation, but it enables the enemy to act secretly or openly in such a way that measures which might deal him a decisive blow are either never taken or are indefinitely delayed.

Chapter 6

DEFENSE OF THE TERRITORY

Since the stake in *modern warfare* is the control of the populace, the first objective is to assure the people their protection by giving them the means of defending themselves, especially against terrorism.

We then have to create and train organizations capable of detecting the elements our enemies will strive to introduce into our territory preparatory to the open struggle.

Finally, if hostilities break out, if terrorism and guerrilla activity have established themselves over a large portion of our territory, we must combat them with the appropriate methods, which will be far more effective than those which would have been considered and used in peacetime.

THE INHABITANTS' ORGANIZATION

Military schools teaching classic doctrines of warfare rely upon a number of decision factors—the mission, the enemy, the terrain, and the resources.

But one factor that is essential to the conduct of *modern warfare* is omitted—the inhabitant.

The battlefield today is no longer restricted. It is limitless; it can encompass entire nations. The inhabitant in his home is the center of the conflict. Amidst the continuing movement of military actions, he is the stablest element. Like it or not, the two camps are compelled to make him participate in the combat; in a certain sense, he has become a combatant also. Therefore, it is essential to prepare him for the role he will have to play and to enable him to fulfill it effectively on our side.

For the inhabitant to elude the threats of the enemy, to cease to be an isolated target that no police force can protect, we must have him participate in his own defense. To this end, we have him enter into a structured organization encompassing the entire population. No one shall be able to avoid this service, and each person at any moment will be subject to the orders of his civil or military superiors to participate in protective measures.

Control of the masses through a tight organization, often through several parallel organizations, is the master weapon of *modern warfare*. This is what permits the enemy to uncover quickly any hostile element within a subjugated population. Only when we have created a similar organization will we be able to discover, and as quickly eliminate, those individuals the enemy tries to introduce among us.

The creation of such an organization may run into serious difficulties, but they are not insurmountable if we firmly desire to succeed. There will be no lack of good will; danger will create it. The experience of the battle of Algiers provides us with a sound basis for this assumption.

First, we designate an energetic and intelligent man in each city who will, with one or more reliable assistants, build the projected organization with a minimum of help from the authorities.

The principle is very simple. The designated leader divides the city into districts, at the head of each of which he places a chief and two or three assistants. These, in turn, divide the district into sub-districts and designate a chief and several assistants for each of them. Finally, each building or group of houses receives a chief and two or three assistants who will be in direct contact with the populace.

Careful investigation is necessary before designating members of the organization and to prevent failures. Nevertheless, making each member responsible for the designation and control of his immediate subordinates will permit rapid creation of the organization on a sound foundation.

In our overseas territories or during a period of crisis at home, when for a variety of reasons we may not be sure of the loyalty of the people— particularly if the enemy organization previously created is sufficiently strong to oblige the population to walk carefully—the problem will be more complex, since the inhabitants will reject any responsibility that might subject them to the adversary's retaliation.

In this case, the pyramid of our organization is created from the bottom up by the police forces charged with maintaining order. Mobile gendarmerie squadrons, with their accustomed police contacts with the people, will be especially qualified to perform this delicate task.

First, they conduct a careful census of the entire population. The basic leader of the organizational structure will be the head of the family. He is made responsible for all inhabitants of his apartment or house, and for keeping up to date the list established at the time of the census.

During the taking of the census, we designate at the next echelon a chief of a group of houses (or of a building, or a floor of a building), who will be responsible for a certain number of heads of family, four or five at most.

Finally, when the census is completed and a close relationship established with the population, chiefs of sub-districts will be designated. According to the way in which the city is divided up, it will be possible for a sub-district leader to be made responsible for some ten chiefs of house groups. Since this individual will play a key role, the district commander should appoint him and then only after careful investigation. The essential quality of a potential sub-district leader is that he have firm attachments in the sub-district (a business or shop, affluence, a large family). That is, he should have a standard of living or family ties that it would be difficult for him to abandon.

There will be no structural echelon above the sub-district leader. His role is too important for him to be easily commanded, and he will be too vulnerable a target for the enemy. The organization will actually be a pyramid of which the sub-district leader will constitute the apex.

In case of war, a special civil and military organism is set up for an entire medium-sized city or for districts in the larger cities. Its essential role is to transmit orders to the sub-district leaders, to see to their execution, and to gather information the sub-district leaders will provide. Having permanent contact with the sub-district leaders, this special organism will ensure continuing and correct execution of instructions issued to the various echelons of the organization.

The population census will permit each inhabitant to be given a *census card*, one or two copies of which will remain in the possession of the forces of order.

The card will include a photograph of the individual, as well as, say, his house-group number (e.g., 3), the letter of the sub-district (B), the number of the district (2), and the letter designating the city (A). The result will constitute what amounts to a catalog number (A.2.B.3.), which will, in the course of frequent checks, enable us to keep tabs on each individual and on the ability of the leaders upon whom he depends.

This organization will permit the command to enlist the participation of the populace in its own protection. To a certain extent, it will be able to participate in the tasks of the forces of order and carry out simple police missions. Detection, surveillance, and occasionally the arrest of dangerous individuals will be managed without difficulty, and the transmission of instruction will always be easy and quick. The organization will rapidly become one of the essential elements of the territorial command and will assume an ever increasing importance. A special office, which we shall call the *bureau of the inhabitants' organization and control,* will be necessary to monitor the organization's activity.

In case of emergency, this organism would be in a position to establish without delay very strict control over food supplies, animals, and all resources our adversaries could use against us. This organization will enable the precise identification of the outlaw: Any individual who is slow to establish himself and does not enter the organization would, in effect, be an outlaw.

A careful search of the population is necessary to find men capable of being leaders of the organization at its various echelons. The bulk of the population is by habit or tradition normally devoted to established authority and the forces of order. The people will be ready to help if we ask their aid, on the condition that we will at all times support and protect those who are on our side. This protection is one of the essential missions of the inhabitants' organization.

Good will is never lacking even in the most troubled of times. Indochina and, later, Algeria have amply proven this. But we ought never to forget that ambition has always been a powerful incentive for a young and dynamic elite that wishes to get out of its rut and arrive. It is largely to this youth that we must appeal. We must bind them to us and compensate services rendered according to their worth.

Finally, of course, we may always assure ourselves of their loyalty by placing them within an organization it will be difficult to leave once admitted.

This inhabitants' organization certainly runs counter to our traditional spirit of individualism and may promote dangers to our liberties that we must not minimize. The analogy with certain totalitarian organizations will afford our adversaries easy opportunities to attack us.

But we cannot permit ourselves to be deluded. There is a fundamental difference. Our organization is a defensive one, the sole aim of which is to ensure the protection of the populace, particularly against the danger of terrorism. No individual entering it need abdicate a particle of his basic liberties; but in the face of a common enemy, each will give under discipline his total and unreserved assistance to his fellows and his superiors. Once the war is won or the danger has passed, our organization will have no reason to exist.

Abuses are always possible. The organization will have to be seriously controlled, so that it remains solely a means of protection against the external enemy and does not become a vehicle for internal political pressure. This cannot happen if it is created in a spirit of justice and if the burdens it necessitates are equitably shared among all the inhabitants of a given region, no matter what their social circumstances may be.

One should not lose sight of the fact that this is the sole means we have to assure the protection of peaceful citizens and to prevent terrorism from forcing them into a harsh and inhuman servitude.

Formerly, nations spent huge sums for the construction of fortifications designed to protect themselves against invasion. Today, the inhabitants' organization, the elite formation designed as a framework for protection and to give us information about the enemy's clandestine penetration of our territory, constitutes the modern means of defense against *modern warfare*.

Any country that does not create such an organization runs a permanent danger of being invaded. The financial outlays called for cannot be compared with those needed for the construction of elaborate fortifications. We have no excuse if we do not create such an organization.

COUNTRYWIDE INTELLIGENCE

With a reliable intelligence service, we would be able to detect all infiltration attempts against our territory and to discover who are those indispensable to the enemy's preparation of his projected offensive action.

The inhabitants will know them, since they suffer terribly from their activities, but will not denounce these agents unless they can do so without risk. Fear of reprisal will always prevent them from communicating to us information they possess.

The inhabitants' organization, which in large measure assures their security, will therefore be an important organism for information. In its very creation, it passes the entire population through a sieve and learns the circumstances in which each person lives. Contacts are made, and a certain confidence in the forces of order established.

Then, frequent meetings of responsible leaders at various echelons will permit regular and frequent relations between the authorities and qualified representatives of the people. Much information will also be gathered, the source of which our adversaries will not succeed in discovering. We will thus have created an initial element of security and understanding.

We cannot hope to transform all the inhabitants into agents. But since *modern warfare* asserts its presence on the totality of the population, we have to be everywhere informed. Therefore, we must have a vast intelligence network, which ought to be set up, if possible, before the opening of hostilities.

During a period of crisis, we complain of not being better informed. We accuse the people unjustly of concealing the truth or of not giving us the information they possess. And very often, because we have not prepared anything, we will be tempted to obtain by violence information that a well-organized service would have given us without difficulty.

Selective terrorism, as we have seen, will, even before the opening of hostilities, put an end to our regular intelligence agents. Leaders and small functionaries are its first victims. The threat of the enemy's warfare organization quickly condemns the population to silence. When hostilities begin, we shall be cut off precipitously from all sources of information if we have made no provision to guard against it.

Even before the inhabitants have been organized, we ought to give a portion of the populace the chance of informing us securely. The time is past when a specialized service could recruit a few agents haphazardly and from a quite special sector of society.

We have to have numerous and secretly established centers of accelerated training, where we will be able to train quickly a great number of inhabitants in the agent roles we shall ask them to play. Their training will be essentially practical: It will be limited to teaching them a few elementary procedures for transmitting simple information (telephone, letter box, dead-drop, etc.), which will be sufficient to ensure their protection.

We then distribute them throughout all phases of human activity—factories, yards, administrative offices, the large public services—everywhere people gather we will be present, thanks to them. We shall almost always be able to recruit them in the very circles of interest to us; if not, we shall get them jobs appropriate to their professional or vocational aptitudes that will serve them as cover.

These "benevolent" agents can give us information on their milieu and inform us of the agents the enemy attempts to infiltrate into the population—that is, such basic activists as fund collectors, propagandists, strike leaders, etc., who usually constitute the first echelon of the opponent's organization. Working among them, often in their very midst, our agents can discover them without difficulty.

This intelligence network, despite its extent and the considerable number of agents it will put to work, can be created at little expense. Their employment itself will provide the agents with a steady income. Various premiums for production will usually be sufficient to sustain their enthusiasm.

Information is nothing in itself, particularly during a crisis, if it is not quickly exploited. Therefore, we must create an intelligence-action service capable of exploiting its own information in the shortest possible time.

Certain individuals of our broadly based intelligence system, after proving their exceptional qualities, will be able to enter the intelligence-action service. They ought to be capable of detecting, following, and sometimes even arresting the enemy agents they uncover.

But our best agents will be furnished to us by the enemy himself. During the course of interrogations, we should always bear in mind that the majority of individuals arrested, if we have enough flexibility, can change camp. Many among them have passed over to the service of the enemy only through duress and have been kept there solely by a continuing threat of blackmail. If we generously offer them another path with our protection, they will become our most faithful collaborators.

As for others, it will suffice to lead them to denounce openly members of the organization whom they know, particularly their superiors and their subordinates. From then on, they are no longer able to betray us and will collaborate with us if only to assure their own protection.

Finally, experience has demonstrated that, although confessions and conversions may be difficult to obtain at lower echelons, they are, at a higher level, and especially among intellectuals, usually easy and quick.

It is thus that we shall recruit the basic agents of our *intelligence-action* service. Well trained by specialists of the forces of order, they will themselves be prepared to exploit their own information in the destruction of the opposing organization.

But, except for a few individuals capable of playing a double-agent role, profitable use of them is of short duration. We shall have to renew them frequently, particularly after all their information has been exploited.

This service should cooperate with all the elements charged with exploiting leads, be prepared to follow closely all police operations, and be *au courant* of all arrests so as to utilize to the maximum all recruitment possibilities.

A well-organized intelligence service can make us aware of the structure of the warfare organization our opponents seek to implant upon our territory.

The most effective solution would no doubt consist of destroying these opponents before they constitute a danger. However, if for various reasons—in general, political ones—we are not authorized to do this, we ought to observe their development closely so as to be in a position to arrest them the moment the order is given.

The best way to be well informed consists in introducing our own agents into the organization of the enemy and in corrupting his agents. This is a delicate task that only a few proven agents will be able to accomplish.

As the adversary's organization begins to expand, our opponents, working in an enemy country, will find that their freedom of action becomes more limited. They run into increasing difficulties as they recruit more and more persons; they are no longer able to exercise tight control over all their agents. Then we will have the opportunities of introducing our own agents into their organization, and we ought to exploit them.

Here again, the best candidates will be furnished to us by the enemy himself. The security of a clandestine organization is assured by rigorous compartmentation. Personal contacts are, for reasons of security, rare at higher echelons. A well-trained intelligence-action service should be able to make frequent arrests of members of the enemy organization in utmost secrecy. We should try to make them pass quickly into our service, permitting them to remain within their own organization after having established a sure system of communications.

We should not underestimate our adversaries, nor should we overestimate them and attribute to them powers they do not possess. They, too, will always have innumerable difficulties to overcome. The thing that makes their task easy is the absence of a special service created to combat them, and the practically total freedom we permit them in the field of clandestinity.

If we prepare ourselves in peacetime to face *modern warfare,* if we provide the people with a means of defending themselves, if we take precautions to be informed at all times of the preparations and the intentions of our adversaries, then we shall have no difficulty in quickly taking the necessary action when the time comes to reduce our adversaries to impotence.

This capability will not go unnoticed; in itself, it may be sufficient to discourage any attempt at a trial of force and serve to maintain the peace. If, however, our adversaries should decide to pass over to open warfare, we would have at hand the means of crushing any enemy who attempts to carry the war onto our territory.

But if the measures decribed above are not adopted, our adversaries will be able to undertake an open struggle to attain their final objective, which is *to overthrow the established authority and to replace it with their own system.*

Since it is the population that is at stake, the struggle will assume two aspects: Political—direct action on the population; and military—the struggle against the armed forces of the aggressor. Our adversaries will not open hostilities until a certain number of preliminary conditions have been realized. By that time their infiltration of our position will be profound and extensive. It will be possible to eradicate it only by powerful means, a firm intention to prevail, and a considerable investment in time.

Part Two

THE POLITICAL AND MILITARY CONDUCT OF THE WAR

I. THE POLITICAL ASPECT

Chapter 7

DIRECT ACTION ON THE POPULATIONS OF CITIES

Internal warfare within a population, particularly in cities, generally involves an extensive *police operation.* There is also an intensive *propaganda effort,* destined primarily to make the steps that are taken understood. A broad *social program* follows, the objective of which is to give the people the material and moral assistance necessary to permit them to resume their normal activities quickly after operations are over.

We have seen how action against the population is conducted by the enemy, and we stressed the primary role of terrorism supported by a warfare organization.

Any actions taken in cities against enemy organizations will be essentially broad *police operations* and will be performed by the regular police forces if these are adequate and capable. If not, the army may take over the task.

The mission of the police operation is not merely to seek a few individuals who have carried out terrorist attacks, but to eliminate from the midst of the population the entire enemy organization that has infiltrated it and is manipulating it at will.

Simultaneously, units of the army will spread their activity throughout the entire city, throwing over it an immense net to overlay the police forces already in place. The police organization will not be disturbed, but will continue to operate within its normal framework while cooperating completely with the army.

Without fear of reaction from the enemy, the army will operate in light detachments. A highly mobile reserve element, the size of a company, will usually allow the handling of any unforeseen eventuality in even a large city.

The police forces can take advantage of the army's presence and the protection and assistance that it will afford to undertake without delay (as described in the preceding chapter) the organization and control of the population, the creation of a broadly based intelligence service, and the establishment of an intelligence-action service—all of which ought to start functioning as quickly as possible.

In this way, we can oppose the enemy with our own organization. If we are serious, it will quickly be in place. Working openly in a systematic way and with great resources, the forces of order will often be able to outrun the enemy, who, obliged to operate in secret, has only limited resources at his disposal.

Then, in collaboration with the police services, we obtain as much information as possible on the organization to be destroyed and then reconstruct, if possible, its organizational chart. Since it is adapted to each city according to the city's importance and the local situation, the organization will rarely be very different in its general structure from that of Algiers in 1956–57, described at the beginning of this study.

The forces of order must simultaneously initiate normal police operations, which from the outset will run into serious difficulties. We know that if the enemy opens hostilities it is because certain preliminary conditions have been met: Principally, he is capable of exercising a strong hold over the populace his attacks have terrorized.

The people know certain key persons in the enemy organization—fund collectors, activists, and terrorists of the armed groups who live in permanent contact with the population. But they will not denounce them unless they can do so in safety. Therefore, assuring this safety is one of the first aims of the inhabitants' organization and the intelligence service. We cannot wait, however, until an intelligence network has been set up before obtaining from the population the information we need. Operations must begin as soon as the army has taken up its position.

The inhabitants are first mustered entirely, by city district. They are quickly interrogated, individually and in secret, in a series of previously arranged small rooms. Any noncommissioned officer of the unit can ask them simple questions, the most frequent of which will be, "Who in your district collects the organization's funds?"

As time goes on, we increase the number of interrogation teams. Certain inhabitants, assured that their identities will not be disclosed, will readily give the information requested. After verifying this data, we proceed to the arrest of the individuals who have been singled out. In this manner, we can capture the first-echelon elements of the enemy organization.

Except for rare cases of emergency, the arrests should take place at night, facilitated by a curfew. The forces of order can easily watch all the streets of a city with a minimum of troops. Anyone found away from his home at night is suspect, and will be arrested and interrogated. Numerous small patrols will move about rapidly and securely apprehend most of the individuals sought in their homes. These are interrogated on the spot by specialized teams. They must give quickly the names and addresses of their superiors, so that the latter may be arrested before the lifting of the curfew. During the day, they would surely be forewarned and would place themselves beyond our reach. A series of night raids will cause important elements of the enemy organization to fall into our hands and will disrupt it.

There are other effective intelligence and control procedures. When we arrest important leaders, we carefully disguise them and line up before them all persons picked up in the course of police raids. The leaders will be able to point out members of their organization they recognize, whom we can arrest on the spot. At other times, we may place the leaders in concealed "observation posts," set up at heavily trafficked points in a city, from which they will indicate (by radio or other means) recognized individuals to surveillance teams who will quickly apprehend them.

One of our most effective methods is the census card (already described) issued to each individual. Of course, the important members of the enemy organization always have one or more pseudonyms, but certain inhabitants have met them at one time or other, although they may not know their name, function, or place of residence. However, they can readily recognize them from the photographs on the copies of the census card retained by the authorities. At one time, we can obtain not only their exact address, but also the names of those who are responsible for their movements (chiefs of house-groups and chiefs of sub-districts).

But the conduct of a police operation in the middle of a city raises numerous difficulties. We should note the main ones so that we may be able to overcome them.

1. *Modern warfare* is a new experience for the majority of our fellow citizens. Even among our friends, the systematic conduct of raids will run into opposition, resulting generally from a total lack of understanding of the enemy and his methods of warfare. This will often be very difficult to overcome.

For example, the fact that the enemy's warfare organization in a single city may consist of several thousand men will come as a surprise even to the majority of high administrative functionaries, who thought sincerely that they were dealing with only a few isolated criminals.

One of the first problems encountered, that of lodging the individuals arrested, will generally not have been anticipated. Prisons, designed essentially to accommodate offenders against common law, will rapidly become inadequate and will not meet our needs. We will be compelled to intern the prisoners under improvised, often deplorable conditions, which will lead to justifiable criticism our adversaries will exploit. From the beginning of hostilities, prison camps should be set up according to the conditions laid down by the Geneva Convention. They should be sufficiently large to take care of all prisoners until the end of the war.

2. By every means—and this is a quite legitimate tactic—our opponents will seek to slow down and, if possible, put an end to our operations. The fact that a state of war will generally not have been declared will be, as we have already indicated, one of their most effective means of achieving this. In particular, they will attempt to have arrested terrorists treated as ordinary criminals and to have members of their organization considered as minor peacetime offenders.

On this subject, the files of the Algiers terrorist organization divulged some particularly interesting documents.

"We are no longer protected by legality," wrote the chief of the Algiers F.L.N. in 1957, when the army had taken over the functions of the police. "We ask all our friends to do the impossible to have legality re-established; otherwise we are lost."

Actually, the peacetime laws gave our enemies maximum opportunities for evading pursuit; it was vital to them that legality be strictly applied. The appeal was not launched in vain. Shortly thereafter, a violent press campaign was unleashed, both in France and abroad, demanding that peacetime laws be strictly adhered to in the course of police operations.

3. Warfare operations, especially those of a police nature in a large city, take place in the very midst of the populace, almost in public, whereas formerly they occurred on a battlefield, to which only armed forces had access.

Certain harsh actions can easily pass for brutalities in the eyes of a sensitive public. And it is a fact also that, in the process of extirpating the terrorist organization from their midst, the people will be manhandled, lined up, interrogated, searched. Day and night, armed soldiers will make unexpected intrusions into the homes of peaceful citizens to carry out necessary arrests. Fighting may occur in which the inhabitants will suffer.

People who know our adversaries will not protest in submitting to inconveniences they know to be necessary for the recovery of their liberty. But our enemies will not fail to exploit the situation for their propaganda needs.

Nevertheless, even if some brutality is inevitable, rigorous discipline must always be enforced to prevent wanton acts. The army has the means of demanding and maintaining firm discipline. It has at its disposal its own system of justice, precisely created to check quickly misdeeds or crimes committed by military personnel in the exercise of their duties. The army must apply the law without hesitation.

Under no pretext, however, can a government permit itself to become engaged in a polemic against the forces of order in this respect, a situation that can benefit only our adversaries.

Police action will therefore be actual operational warfare. It will be methodically pursued until the enemy organization has been entirely annihilated. It will not end until we have organized the population and created an efficient intelligence service to enable it to defend itself. This organization will have to be maintained until the end of hostilities to prevent any return by the enemy to the offensive. After the battle of Algiers in 1957, the French Government, under pressure from our adversaries, permitted the dismantling of everything the army had built up. Three years later, the enemy was able to re-establish his organization and once again to take control of the population (December, 1960). The victory of Algiers in 1957 had gone for naught.

Our war aims must be clearly known to the people. They will have to be convinced that if we call upon them to fight at our sides it can only be in defense of a just cause. And we should not deceive them. The surest means of gaining their confidence will be to crush those who want to oppress them. When we have placed the terrorists out of harm's way, the problem of pacification will be quickly resolved.

As long as we have not arrived at such a point, any *propaganda,* any solution, however skillful, will be ineffective on a populace infected by clandestine organisms that penetrate like a cancer into its midst and terrorize it. It is only when we have delivered it from this evil that it will freely listen, think, and express itself. A just peace will then be quite possible.

During the period of active operations, the role of propaganda action of the masses will have little effect. It will usually be limited to making the people understand that the frequently severe measures taken have no purpose other than to cause the rapid destruction of the enemy.

With the gradual return to peace, however, propaganda will play an important role in causing the sometimes impatient masses to understand the variety of problems that must be resolved before a return to normal existence is possible. The inhabitants' organization will be the most effective instrument of propaganda contact and dissemination.

The people know instinctively what is correct. It is only by substantive measures that we will lead them to judge the validity of our action.

War has always been a calamity for the people. Formerly, only those inhabitants who found themselves in the paths of the armies had to suffer the calamity. Today, *modern warfare* strikes the entire population of a country, the inhabitants of the large cities as well as those of the most remote rural districts.

The enemy, infiltrated among the people, will always try to deprive the inhabitants of their means of subsistence. It is among the people that combat operations will take place, and their activities will be limited in many ways. They will have to suffer the exacting demands the enemy invokes to compel obedience, as well as the frequently severe measures the forces of order are led to take.

It will be the role of the *social services* to lessen the miseries war engenders.

But we must not lose sight of the fact that any material aid we give will only profit the enemy if the organization that permits his control and manipulation of the people has not first been destroyed. Aid must be prudently administered until the police operation has been completed; premature, uncontrolled assistance would be of no use to the inhabitants.

Once peace has been established, even in a small part of the territory, extensive and generous social assistance will be of prime importance in bringing to our cause many people who are unhappy and often disoriented by the military operations and who will not have always understood the underlying reasons for them.

The conduct of military operations in a large city, in the midst of the populace, without the benefit of the powerful weapons it possesses, is certainly one of the most delicate and complex problems ever to face an army.

To carry out effective police work, conduct operations among the citizenry, and cause the inhabitants to participate actively on its side, are obviously tasks for which the military generally has not been prepared. Some feel that these operations should be entirely carried out by the police, and that the army should keep to the nobler task, better adapted to its specialty, of reducing armed bands in the field.

This is a grave error into which our adversaries would certainly like to lead us. The job of the police is only to ensure the protection of the people in time of peace against ordinary offenders or criminals. But the police do not have the means of conducting combat operations against a powerful enemy organization whose aim is not to attack individuals protected by the police, but rather to conquer the nation and to overthrow its regime.

The protection of the national territory and regime is quite clearly the essential role of the army. By and large it has the means necessary for victory; there is only the question of will and method.

II. THE MILITARY ASPECT

Chapter 8

ERRORS IN FIGHTING THE GUERRILLA

The basic weapon of *modern warfare,* particularly in the cities, is terrorism, supported by a special organization. In the countryside, there is an old method of combat that has proved itself in the past and has been taken over and adapted to conditions of *modern warfare:* It is guerrilla warfare, which is rooted in terrorism.

The guerrilla and terrorism are only one stage of *modern warfare,* designed to create a situation favorable to the build-up of a regular army for the purpose of eventually confronting an enemy army on the battlefield and defeating him.

The goal of the guerrilla, during what can be a long period of time, is not so much to obtain local successes as it is to create a climate of insecurity, to compel the forces of order to retire into their most easily defensible areas. This results in the abandonment of certain portions of territory that the guerrillas are then able to control. At the beginning of hostilities, the guerrillas show themselves only in minor but violent actions, which they carry out by surprise but with care to avoid losses.

Dispersion is a necessary part of their defense. Their subsequent regrouping and transformation into large, regularly organized units is not possible until they have acquired absolute control of a vast area in which they are able to secure the substantial material aid necessary for the establishment, training, and enlistment of a regular army.

The appearance of regular units in certain regions does not mean the end of the guerrilla. He will continue actively wherever the establishment of regular units has not been carried out. Regular units and guerrilla bands will cooperate closely to try to bring about a situation favorable to the engagement of the enemy army in a decisive fight to annihilate it.

Modern warfare, like classical wars of the past, will definitely end only with the crushing of one of the two armies on the battlefield, or by capitulation of one side to the war aims of the opponent.

The origin, evolution, and efficacy of the guerrilla are well known. Many authors have studied him, particularly in the various theaters of operation of World War II. He was unquestionably a success in Russia, France, and Yugoslavia. In China and Indochina, it was possible to lead him to a final victory over well-equipped regular modern armies. In Algeria, despite his meager resources of personnel and materiel, he has for years fought a French army that has not succeeded in eliminating him.

There are those who think that, to defeat the guerrilla, it is sufficient to fight him with his own weapons; that is, to oppose the guerrilla with the counterguerrilla. In a way, this is what we tried to do in Indochina and then in Algeria. But the guerrilla's weapons and those of a regular army are quite different, even opposed, in a number of respects.

To attempt to employ guerrilla tactics that we ourselves do not have or cannot put to use is to condemn ourselves to neglect those that we do possess and that can have a definite, useful application.

I believe that the errors committed and the failures sustained flow in large part from confusion between the guerrilla's potential and that of a regular army. For brief intervals in Indochina, we were able to play the part of the counterguerrilla against the Vietminh, and even that of the guerrilla. This experience illustrated the difference between the potential of the guerrilla and of the regular army soldier.

At the time that the French Army occupied Than-Uyen on the right bank of the Red River, to the north of Nghia-Lo in Thai country, the town and its airfield were defended by a fortified post atop a rocky peak, held by one regular company reinforced by some partisans. But its security was rather chancy, even around the immediate approaches of the town, and on numerous occasions the Vietminh were able to open fire on the planes parked on the airfield.

After the fall of Nghia-Lo, the town of Than-Uyen, which had been evacuated by air-lift, was occupied by the Vietminh.

Then, in October, 1953, native maquisards from the right bank of the Red River, recruited from among people who had remained loyal to us, were able with their own resources to reoccupy the Phong-Tho region and its airfield, to launch a successful raid on Lao-Kay, and, finally, to seize Than-Uyen and hold it for seven months, deep behind enemy lines. When observers came back to the town, they were struck by the fact that the fortified post had not been reoccupied and the airfield was never guarded.

Nonetheless, security was tighter than the previous year when French troops held the position.

The regular troops had observed the airfield and its immediate approaches from the fortified post. Outside of a quite limited circle of vision, they were blind, particularly at night when they missed everything. The Vietminh, who knew the limits of this circle, were able to harass us easily.

Our maquisards, recruited from among and living in the midst of the local population, watched not the airfield, but rather the Vietminh themselves. They placed their agents everywhere—in units of the Vietminh, in every village, in every house, and on all the trails of the area. The entire population was responsible for watching the enemy, and nothing could escape its observation. When the maquisards signaled us that the area was free, our planes were able to land without risk on the airfield, to which it was unnecessary to give close protection.

The support of the population is essential to the guerrilla. In particular, it prevents him from being taken by surprise, a vital factor for success in combat. As long as this support is not withdrawn from him, we cannot surprise him, unless he commits some blunder, which is unlikely if he is well trained and battle-hardened.

This is the reason why methods currently employed against guerrillas—such as military outposts, autonomous commando groups or patrols detached from such posts, isolated ambushes, and wide-ranging sweeps—only rarely achieve the hoped-for results, and then usually by accident.

Military outposts, installed at great expense in areas to be pacified, are in general not successful. Often the villages they surround are as well controlled by our enemies as villages quite distant.

Outposts are usually placed at communications junctions that must be held to secure heavy equipment. They cause the guerrillas no trouble because there is no need to take them. Armed bands can freely circulate in the large areas between the outposts, and can organize and control the population without interference. A few cleverly planned terrorist attacks can suffice to subject the inhabitants to their will.

In addition, the disposition of the outposts is an open book to our enemies, who observe them at their leisure. They miss nothing.

The only usefulness of the outposts is the obligation they create for us. To maintain them forces us to open and keep up roads, to protect supply convoys during the course of long hauls, and in general to carry on military activity in which we would not indulge if it were not for the outposts.

To break the feeling of isolation, which is not long in coming, the more active or experienced outposts send out patrols rarely exceeding about sixty men (two platoons) in strength. Certain sectors even make use of specially trained commandos of company strength. Their mission is to patrol day and night a predetermined sector by a variety of routes, with the objective of creating a sense of insecurity in the guerrillas surrounding the post and of reassuring the people by their presence.

The populace sees the commandos or patrols passing through, and often views them sympathetically. But the patrols always pass too quickly to destroy the organization the rebels have set up in each village to terrorize the inhabitants and to bend them to their will—the fund collectors, organization leaders, lookouts, etc. As long as this structure is not demolished, the population's fear will remain the same and the task of pacification can make no headway.

Away from their outposts or bases, the commandos or patrols are unable to subsist for long—a few days at best, just time enough to use up the rations they can carry. They cannot live off the land, because they do not have at their disposal the resources the guerrillas use. The guerrilla bands have inhabitants to guide them, an organization that prepares their bivouac each day, sees to their provisioning, and assures their security.

The commandos move about blindly, guided only by the reconnaissance elements they send ahead. At night, even with sentinels nearby, their security is precarious at best. Physical and mental wear and tear come rapidly.

In addition, they are unable to vary their itinerary as much as they would like, particularly on the trip back and if the terrain is difficult. They cannot escape the observation of the inhabitants and the lookouts, who are able to analyze their habits quickly. They will shortly realize that a patrol on a certain path will not leave it—sometimes by force of habit, often because it has no way of getting out. Nothing will happen as long as our enemies are unable to bring together sufficient forces for an attack. But when this time comes, they will make the best of it.

Patrol action, unwearyingly attempted by military men who still believe it possible to beat the enemy on his own ground, is often rewarded by serious failures; at best, it never produces convincing results.

That is why outposts, when first established, attempt to carry out some external activity, but then pull in their horns and never try again.

For the same reasons, *isolated ambushes* do not accomplish anything. Usually they are betrayed before they take place and come to nothing; at other times, they actually do us harm.

Pursuit commandos or isolated ambushes are combat operations the guerrilla can employ with the backing of the population and when he has a support organization on the spot. As long as we are unable to resort to the same methods, we will achieve only mediocre results, which are disproportionate to the risks run and the efforts demanded from the soldiers.

Large-unit sweeps, conducted with conventional resources within a framework similar to that of conventional warfare, and invariably limited in time,[1] temporarily disperse guerrilla bands rather than destroy them.

A normal operation of this type usually consists in the attempted surprise encirclement of a well-defined zone in which guerrillas are thought to be located, while mobile elements conduct a mopping-up operation. Despite the ingenuity, even mastery, which some commanders have demonstrated in moving their units about, these operations are always the same.

Surprise, that essential factor of success, is practically never realized. As we have seen, the people among whom our troops live and move have as their mission the informing of the guerrillas, and no movement of troops can escape them. The noose is never completely tightened. The troops charged with the mop-up operations are always too few in number to search a vast and difficult terrain in which the dispersed bands are able to disappear during the brief operation.

Traditionally attracted by the purely military aspect of warfare—that is, by the pursuit and destruction in combat of guerrilla bands on the ground—operational commanders invariably hope to succeed in maneuvering them like regular units and to gain a rapid and spectacular success. They have little interest in the less noble task, however essential, of subtle work with the population and the destruction of the clandestine organization that enables guerrilla bands to survive despite local defeats the forces of order periodically inflict.

Only a long occupation of the countryside, which will permit police operations among the people analogous to those carried out in the cities, can succeed.

The certainty of never running the risk of a clear defeat, such as an equally armed opponent could inflict upon us, enables any military commander to conduct some sort of operation. Even if guerrilla bands are not destroyed, at least geographical objectives are secured within the prescribed time, and a few dead rebels will always balance the account. If, moreover, a few arms are recovered, the operation, which has been carried out like a normal peacetime maneuver, then assumes an air of battle and victory sufficient to satisfy a commander who is not too exacting.

But that which is essential—*the destruction of the enemy's potential for warfare*—is never accomplished, principally because it is never seriously contemplated.

If it is still necessary to remove any illusion regarding the possibility of conducting a surprise envelopment against guerrillas, under conditions where the population has not yet been brought under control by the forces of order, an account by a former officer in Indochina follows:

In 1948, in a certain sector, I was able to establish relations with a Vietminh captain in charge of a command (a *Bo Doi*) that was independent of the enemy regiment stationed in the region. He himself was not a Communist, although the entire cadre of the regiment was. Still, he was unwilling to rally to the French cause, and he explained his reasons as follows: "Some day, sooner or later, we shall have peace with France. My personal situation at that time will be what I have made it. If I should go over to your side today, you would always consider me a turncoat, and you would give me at best rather menial employment. I have chosen the Vietminh because it is here that I have the best chances for advancement. If the regiment on my flank, therefore, should suffer a serious defeat, my own sector will increase in importance, and my future will be enhanced. I am in a position to give you information that will be useful to you in this respect."

As a matter of fact, he provided me with a precisely detailed plan of the regimental command post and its camouflaged forest installations, which had previously evaded our observation. In exchange, I generously promised to warn him in advance of the projected operation. "That's quite unnecessary," he said ironically. "I'm always aware of your operations at least twenty-four hours in advance. There will be plenty of time for me to withdraw to another sector."

I had always been convinced that I was preparing my operations in the utmost secrecy, but nothing could escape the numerous agents among the population surrounding us, who spied upon us unceasingly.

NOTE

1. Frequently, in fact, it is decided a priori that a given operation not last more than a short, predetermined time—several days, for example.

Chapter 9

THE PROBLEM OF RESOURCES

The traditional army, having at its disposal large numbers of trained troops and an abundance of modern materiel, in the final analysis is completely incapable of overcoming a practically destitute enemy whose leaders and men have received only rudimentary military training. Incredible as this seems, it is nonetheless a bitter reality.

A slave to its training and traditions, our army has not succeeded in adapting itself to a form of warfare the military schools do not yet teach. Its valiant efforts, sufferings, and sacrifices serve to obstruct the enemy, to slow down the execution of his plan, but they have been incapable of stopping the enemy from attaining his objective.

The army usually strikes into a vacuum, and fruitlessly expends considerable materiel. Nor would a significant increase in materiel bring a solution any closer. It is how we exploit our resources that we must completely revise.

If we want to meet the guerrilla successfully and to defeat him within a reasonable period of time, we must study his methods, study our own methods and their potential, and draw from this study some general principles that will permit us to detect the guerrilla's weak points and concentrate our main efforts on them.

The following table compares simply the guerrilla's basic resources with those of the traditional army:

Traditional army	Guerrilla band
1. Has large numbers of well-armed troops, ready supplies of food and ammunition.	1. Has small numbers of poorly armed troops (at least at the beginning of hostilities), difficulty in obtaining supplies of food and ammunition.
2. Can move quickly over favorable terrain (aviation, motor vehicles, boats, etc.).	2. Can move only on foot.
3. Has a well-organized communications network, which gives it great control advantages.	3. Has little long-distance communications equipment (at least at the outset), which leads to difficulties in coordinating operations.

BUT	BUT
1. Experiences great difficulty in moving about guerrilla country; usually has imperfect knowledge of the terrain.	1. Chooses own terrain, is well adapted to it, can move quickly, and quite often disappears into it.
2. Has practically no support from the population, even if it is not hostile.	2. Has the support of the population (either spontaneous or through terror), to which it is closely tied.
3. Has great difficulty in getting information on the movements and intentions of the guerrilla.	3. Gets information on all our movements from the populace and sometimes (through agents infiltrated into our midst) on our intentions as well.

By studying this table, we can see that the guerrilla's greatest advantages are his perfect knowledge of an area (which he himself has chosen) and its potential, and the support given him by the inhabitants.

The advantages of the traditional army are imposing superiority in numbers and in materiel, practically unlimited sources of supply, and the advantages of command and extended maneuver granted by modern methods of communication and transport.

What can the guerrilla do with the means he has at his disposal?

He chooses the terrain and imposes it upon us. It is usually inaccessible to heavy and quick-moving equipment, and thus deprives us of the benefit of our modern arms. We are forced to fight on foot, under conditions identical to those of the guerrilla.

On his terrain, which he knows perfectly, he is able to trap us easily in ambushes or, in case of danger, to disappear. On the other hand, if he is an incomparable fighter on his own grounds, or in an area to which he has adapted himself, *the guerrilla loses a great deal of his value in new or unknown terrain.* He also is inclined not to leave his area, but clings to it except in case of absolute necessity, because he knows that away from his own terrain and deprived of his means of support he is only a mediocre fighter.

We have already seen how indispensable the support of the population is to the guerrilla. It is possible for him to exist only where the people give him their unqualified support. He cannot live among a populace he has not previously organized and subjected to his will, because it is from it that he must draw his sustenance and protection.

It is the inhabitant who supplies the guerrilla with his food requirements on an almost daily basis, thereby enabling him to avoid setting up cumbersome supply points—so easily identifiable and difficult to re-establish. It is the inhabitant also who occasionally supplies him with ammunition. The inhabitant contributes to his protection by keeping him informed. Our rest and supply bases are located in the midst of a populace whose essential mission is to keep an eye on them. No troop movement can escape the inhabitant. Any threat to the guerrilla is communicated to him in plenty of time, and the guerrilla can take cover or trap us in profitable ambushes. Sometimes the inhabitant's home is the guerrilla's refuge, where he can disappear in case of danger.

But this total dependence upon terrain and population is also the guerrilla's weak point. We should be able, with our more powerful potential, to make him submit or to destroy him by acting upon his terrain and upon his support—the population.

Knowing that the guerrilla sticks to the area of his choice, we ought resolutely to engage him there. Once we have occupied the terrain, we ought to have the will and the patience to track him down until we have annihilated him. This requires time, and our operations will be long.

We know also that he is less of a fighter away from home. We should therefore devote ourselves to making him forgo the benefit of his terrain by causing him to leave it. Whenever possible, we should interrupt his food supplies, much more important than his supplies of ammunition. Action of this kind often implies political or economic measures that do not always fall within the purview of military leaders, but they should be used whenever possible.

Above all, we must loose the guerrilla's hold on the population by systematically destroying his combat organization. Finally, we must permit the people to participate in their own defense and to protect themselves against any offensive return of the enemy, by having them enter into the structured organization we have already described. Such an organization must be established without delay in areas we control that could be the refuge of armed bands.

To recapitulate our rapid analysis, we have three simple principles to apply in fighting the guerrilla—to cut the guerrilla off from the population that sustains him; to render guerrilla zones untenable; and to coordinate these actions over a wide area and for long enough, so that these steps will yield the desired results.

The fight against the guerrilla must be organized methodically and conducted with unremitting patience and resolution. Except for the rare exception, *it will never achieve spectacular results, so dear to laurel-seeking military leaders.* It is only by means of a sum total of perfectly coordinated, complex measures—which we are going to make an effort to study—that the struggle will, slowly but surely, push the guerrilla to the wall.

Before drawing some practical conclusions about the conduct of operations against the guerrilla, we should examine those the U.S. Army conducted with complete success in Korea. Thanks to a series of methodically conducted operations, the army was able, in a relatively short period of time, to eliminate completely the guerrillas who had installed themselves behind the American lines in 1950.

In an article entitled "Beating the Guerrilla," (*Military Review,* December, 1955), Lieutenant Colonel John E. Beebe, of the faculty of the U.S. Army Command and General Staff College, draws profitable lessons from these operations.

Military operations alone he says, are not sufficient. Counterguerrilla operations have two objectives—the destruction of the guerrilla forces, and the eradication of their influence on the population.

The counterguerrilla plan to prevent the formation of guerrilla units or to destroy them if they have been formed, since it will comprise measures that are political, economic, psychological, administrative, and military, must be prepared at a very high command echelon.

For the conduct of operations against the guerrilla, he recommends that the command post of the counterguerrilla forces be established near the guerrilla zone and that troops penetrate the zone of the guerrilla and install bases of operations there, taking the necessary security precautions. Then a plan of combat and ambush against the guerrillas can be prepared, with the idea in mind of constantly maintaining pressure to deprive them of any chance of resting or of reorganizing and preparing new operations.

This operation will end only when there are no longer any guerrillas in the area. Counterguerrilla operations involve large numbers of soldiers and last many months. In Korea, there were two examples.

Operation Ratkiller, in the mountainous region of southwest Korea, was conducted by three divisions—two Korean and one American—to which was added a police battalion. It lasted three and a half months, from December 1, 1951, until March 16, 1952, during the course of which 11,000 guerrillas were killed and 10,000 taken prisoner.

Operation Trample, against guerrilla elements still remaining in the south of Korea, was conducted by two divisions from December, 1953, until June, 1954—just about six months. It was the last of the operations against the guerrilla, and the first during the course of which the population gave its total support to the troops responsible for the maintenance of order.

These lessons do not differ from those that may be drawn from several successful counterguerrilla operations in South Vietnam, at the beginning of the Indochina campaign, and even in Algeria.

Chapter 10

CONDUCTING COUNTERGUERRILLA OPERATIONS

THE ENEMY ORGANIZATION

In any military operation, we must first locate the enemy before we can concentrate our blows against him.

We know that in *modern warfare* we are not clashing with just a few armed bands, but rather with an organization installed within the population—an organization that constitutes the combat machine of the enemy, of which the bands are but one element.

To win, we have to destroy this entire organization.

We have seen the importance the *organization* can assume in a single city like Algiers. And because of our experience in Algeria, we know what a war organization covering a whole country is like.

Algeria is divided into 6 *wilayas* (major military districts); each *wilaya* is divided into 4 or 5 zones; each zone into 4 or 5 regions; each region into 4 or 5 sectors; and, finally, each sector is divided into a certain number of communes.

Just as in the cities, at each geographical level fulfilling the same functions we find the same leaders—a politico-military leader, a political assistant, a military assistant, and an assistant responsible for liaison and intelligence.

There are also departments, unnecessary in the cities, that have been created for the broader organization—a director responsible for logistical problems, especially for food supplies; and a person responsible for the health service, for organizing hospitals when possible, and for looking after the populace in this respect.

The councils at all levels make their decisions in common, but the politico-military leader has the deciding voice.

(The geographic breakdown, made solely with the conduct of the war in mind, is never patterned on the lines of peacetime administration. Nevertheless, the approximate equivalents are as follows: A *wilaya* comprises the same area as an *igamie*,[1] a zone that of a French department, and a region that of an arrondissement.)

The *basic* unit of organization is the region. It is the lowest echelon at which a complete staff, such as we have just described, is found. At lower levels—the sector and the commune—the staff is merely embryonic. In the communes in particular, it is reduced to the "committee of five," the most important of whom is the man charged with problems of supply.

A region is divided into a certain number of sectors, four or five depending upon the extent of the area and the characteristics of the terrain. (See the adjoining sketch.)

SKETCH OF A THEORETICAL REGION

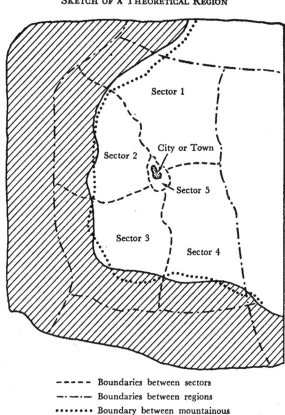

Sector 1

City or Town

Sector 2

Sector 5

Sector 3

Sector 4

‒ ‒ ‒ ‒ Boundaries between sectors
—·—·— Boundaries between regions
•••••••• Boundary between mountainous
and inhabited areas

The urban sector is small in area but encompasses the largest population concentration of the region, quite often the chief town of the arrondissement. Here there is located a military unit the size of a platoon, well trained and well armed, especially entrusted with the task of carrying out assassinations and of continually presenting a threat to the inhabitants of the town. Then there are three or four sectors of similar characteristics. In the urban sector, the enemy permanently assigns some of his own people to serve in the town's political administration. Each is in charge of an area of the inhabited flat land that extends from the town to the hilly country. It is here that the "base" of the armed band is located, usually a company per sector. The *refuge area* is in the roughest part of the adjoining mountains, to which the band may withdraw in case of danger.

Except for operational missions ordered by the region, or in case of grave danger, the band does not leave its sector, where it has its roots and the elements that help it to subsist. Away from its sector, it would enjoy no support and would usually move about in unknown terrain. In such cases, it would be quite vulnerable.

Within a given sector, the various elements of the enemy organization are divided geographically into three groups:

The towns or population centers each under the command of a politico-administrative leader responsible for organizing urban terrorism, collection of funds, propaganda, and an intelligence service, whose main task is to report on the movements of army troops stationed in the town.

The inhabited rural area, under the command of a politico-military leader responsible for maintaining a firm hold on the population; distributing or arranging delivery of supplies coming from the towns, sheltering and feeding the band normally stationed there or those passing through; and providing the bands with information and, thanks to its armed partisans, close protection. In such an area, which is under some sort of control by the forces of order at least sporadically, the politico-military organization plays a very important role.

The refuge area, under the command of a politico-military leader, responsible for seeing to the guerrillas' security and supply, and assuring that the depots and bivouac areas are guarded when the bands are moving about. The refuge area is situated in terrain to which access is difficult, isolated by the cutting of roads, sabotage of bridges, etc.; and so organized to permit the bands to be stationed there.

The armed guerrilla band, because of the permanent threat it poses to the population and the fear it inspires among units of the forces of order, is the guarantee of the entire organization. It normally inhabits the refuge area, but makes frequent visits to the intermediate area between the refuge area and the town, especially in winter when it lives there practically all the time.

The members of the sector organization thus live under one of two different kinds of situation—either in the town and the intermediate area; or in the intermediate or refuge area. But there is no direct connection between the towns and the refuge area.

When such an organization has been able to establish itself in a country, military operations directed against the armed bands never quite reach them. Even if they did reach them, the essential part of the organization would remain in place and, even without the bands, would stay sufficiently powerful to retain its hold over the population.

Victory therefore can be attained only through the complete destruction of the entire organization.

COUNTERGUERRILLA STRATEGY

The most vulnerable part of the enemy organization is in the towns. It is always within the control of the army troops that occupy it, and a police operation conducted along the lines already described can destroy it.

But *the most desirable objective is the destruction of the politico-military organization in the intermediate area.* This we should undertake as soon as we have the necessary means at our disposal. Such an operation will lead us back to the town organization and also provide us with the channel essential to reaching the bands in the refuge areas. We can thus destroy the entire organization supporting the bands. Cut off from their sources of supply and information, they will be more vulnerable.

A broad envelopment, therefore, ought logically to begin with a police operation in the intermediate area. The occupation of the intermediate area and the destruction of the organization supporting the bands is our first objective. In this way we can, in an initial phase, compel the bands to withdraw into the refuge area. Deprived of supplies and information, they will no longer be able to leave without risk and will find it difficult to defend themselves when we finally decide to attack them.

COUNTERGUERRILLA TACTICS

The Organization of Defense: "Gridding"

The enemy's first acts of war—terrorist attacks, localized guerrilla action—generally take the peacetime forces of order—police, gendarmerie, army—by surprise. Too widely dispersed and too vulnerable, these forces quickly fall back upon the built-up areas, which offer them the best chance of resisting the aggressor.

Some elements are pushed back to positions that must be held. Traffic between these held positions is maintained or re-established by means of armed convoys, but the majority of secondary roads are abandoned.

The aggressor also obliges us to take up an area defense to protect vital positions and to prevent complete strangulation of the territory. This defense, more or less in depth, is established after taking into consideration immediate needs and available resources—vulnerable points, population density, attitude of the inhabitants, the necessity of keeping open roads and ways essential to the life of the country.

Eventually there is established a so-called defensive grid system, in which the military organization follows the lines of the civil administration to make maximum use of all command possibilities and to permit normal administration to function insofar as possible—the department becomes a zone, the arrondissement becomes a sector, the canton becomes a *quartier.*

The retreat of the forces of order rapidly delivers a large part of the territory to the enemy. Surprise has been to his advantage. From this point on he will attempt to consolidate and complete his combat organization, to defend the territory he has conquered against the forces of order, to crush one by one the largest number possible of the squares of the grid in order to increase the area under his control.

Offense—Sector Level

How can we, with the forces at our immediate disposal, plus the reinforcements we shall receive, set about the destruction of the enemy's combat organization and the liberation of the occupied territory?

First of all, we have the troops that make up the initial grid, called sector troops. If the region is the basis of the enemy's organization, the sector (arrondissement) is the basis of our system.

The withdrawal of our elements has led to the creation of military posts in the most important villages and in the towns, particularly in the principal town of the sector.

We have observed how ineffective outposts are. Since the control of the population is the aim of *modern warfare,* any element not in direct and permanent contact with the population is useless. Furthermore, if we try to make strongholds of outposts, we would be surrounding them with walls built to support a siege the enemy has neither the intention nor the possibility of undertaking.

In the villages, however, we often find one or two empty houses, where the bands usually stay while in transit, which we can occupy. Other houses for the lodging of the men can be rented from the inhabitants or constructed if necessary.

We then organize not just the defense of a sole military post, but that of the entire village and its inhabitants, making it a strategic hamlet. A tight, impassable perimeter is created (of barbed-wire, underbrush, various other materials), protected by a few armed blockhouses, manned with automatic weapons and capable of covering the whole perimeter.

A police operation is undertaken immediately within the village thus protected. Simultaneously, we organize the population according to the principles we studied previously.

Inhabitants of the nearest villages or isolated individuals are progressively brought within the security perimeter. Most of the others will come there themselves. The inhabitants are allowed to leave the village only by the gates, and all exits will be controlled. They are permitted to take neither money nor supplies with them. No one will be able to leave or enter the village by night.

In effect, we are re-establishing the old system of medieval fortified villages, designed to protect the inhabitants against marauding bands.

The first police operation will be carried out in the principal town of the sector (arrondissement). An office for the *control and organization of the inhabitants* is installed as soon as possible at the sector military staff. The town itself will be surrounded by a tight and protected perimeter, and all its entrances and exits will be controlled.

Inhabitants of the principal town and villages will, as we said earlier, receive a *census card,* a copy of which will be sent to the command post of the sector and district. Each card will bear a photograph of the individual, his house-group number (4), the letter of the sub-district (B), the number of the district (2), and the letter of the town or strategic hamlet (C).

The first part (C2) lets us know where he comes from; the second part (B4) tells us the leaders responsible for the individual—the house-group leader and the sub-district leader. The census card will also enable us to control individual ration cards.

A census is also taken of all animals—draft animals (horses, donkeys, and mules) and bovines (calves, cows, and bulls) will be branded with the card number of their owner. We know how important supplies are to the guerrilla. Henceforth, no supplies are permitted to leave the towns or strategic hamlets. Even the animals will be strictly controlled. If we prohibit uncontrolled traffic of food on the main roads, we can cut off the enemy's main sources of supply in a very short time.

Thus, even with much reduced forces, we can again regain control of the major portion of the country's population—from 80 to 90 per cent, if one considers the total number of inhabitants of the large towns down to villages having gendarme units to control them. In this way, we have in our hands an important mass of people adequately protected and controlled, and able to be used to block the enemy offensive on all sides.

The intervals between the grid squares, however, still remain empty of troops; their defenseless inhabitants are at the mercy of enemy action. Broad-scale operations or commando raids may cause our opponents passing concern, but they are usually too brief and superficial to destroy their combat organization.

The organization and control of the inhabitants of the towns and strategic hamlets permit a majority of them to take part in their own defense. A certain number of troops can in this way be freed to reinforce the reserve element of the sector command. Being unengaged and mobile, they will form the sector's *interval troops* and act continuously between the outposts.

This force should be large enough to outclass an armed band whose size and quality will vary according to the guerrilla's position and circumstances. But if we react quickly enough, before the situation can deteriorate, the enemy will not be able to create bands larger than approximately a company. This is the normal unit that will permit him to move about securely over long distances and to live off the country and the inhabitant, usually his sole sources of supply.

Therefore, a four-company battalion of infantry will be our standard interval unit. It must be essentially mobile, moving usually by foot, but also equipped with vehicles to move quickly over long distances. Its basic mission will be to destroy the politico-military organization in the intermediate area; to destroy the armed bands that attempt to oppose this action, to bring in people to the strategic hamlets and, if possible, to create new hamlets for regrouping and control of every inhabitant of the intermediate area.

If the sector's interval troops do not amount to at least a four-company battalion, they will certainly be unable to handle at one time the intermediate areas of an enemy region, which corresponds approximately to a French sector (arrondissement).

We know that, within the region, each enemy sector has an intermediate area of its own, where it puts up and supports an armed band.

At very least, we must attack the intermediate area of an enemy sector. Its boundaries are easily definable. Our police operations in the towns and strategic hamlets will have yielded sufficient information for us to establish them without difficulty. The interval troops cannot hope to surprise the enemy in this area by stealthy penetration, a desire we have seen is illusory, but they can surprise him by their methods.

Troops penetrate the intermediate area at the ready to avoid being surprised and to be in a position to maneuver in the event of a chance encounter with a band. If the band succeeds in escaping or finds itself in its refuge area, the police operation commences immediately. The politico-military organization does not follow the band, as it would only be excess baggage. It stays in place or in the immediate vicinity. It is therefore always within range of the interval troop units, if there is sufficient time to look for it and destroy it.

Keeping one element in reserve, the troops spread over a large area in order to occupy, if possible, the entire intermediate area of the sector, especially the maximum number of villages and the most frequented paths.

Then, while part of the cadre sets out on an intensive search of the terrain, to locate any caches or deposits and to study a layout for the night's ambushes, the units' specialists undertake the police work.

The entire population of each village, men and women, is called together and prohibited from leaving for the duration of the operation. Every inhabitant is individually and privately interrogated, without any resort to violence. A few simple but precise questions will be asked of each. For the first interrogation, two in general will suffice—Which individuals collect funds in your village? Who are the young people who are armed and carry on the surveillance of the village?

If this first interrogation is well handled, several people will readily make the desired replies. Quite often, since guilty individuals hope to escape detection, the ones we seek will be among those assembled. We will therefore have no difficulty in arresting them. Those who have succeeded in leaving the village will not have gotten very far. Deprived of any contact with the population, they may very likely fall into our night ambushes when they attempt to find out what is going on or try to escape.

The first echelon of the enemy politico-military organization will also fall into our hands. More stringent interrogation will enable us to discover quickly who all the members are—front leaders, members of committees of five, supply people, lookouts, etc.—as well as the location of food deposits and arms caches.

At least a week is needed for the specialized teams to destroy a village politico-military organization. This is likewise the minimum for a police operation in the inhabited rural area of an enemy sector.

Parallel to the work of destruction, we lay the foundation of our own system by selecting intelligence agents and organizing the populace.

To succeed, we must never lose sight of the fact that we will receive information only from people who can give us information without risk to themselves. We must assure our agents of this indispensable security.

We will choose them in the village itself. They will usually be people who proved best informed during the first interrogation. Having marked them, we contact them only in the course of the next police operation and under the same circumstances. They will then point out to us those men the enemy has installed to replace his disrupted organization. Later, when the situation has improved, we can find out who are capable of handling the secret communication of simple information.

We proceed immediately to the organization and control of the population of the intermediate area.

The first resort is the traditional division of the area into districts, subdistricts and house-groups—with the usual numbering. We conduct an exact census of all the inhabitants, their means of subsistence, and in particular their livestock. Then we enroll them in the structured organization of which we have already spoken.

In the beginning, we will not make many demands on the cadres we have chosen. But this initial activity will greatly facilitate the control of the population in the course of subsequent police operations, which must be frequent if we want to prevent the destroyed organization from reconstituting itself. Individuals will be considered suspect who appear in the census but who cannot be found. Their leaders and their families will be held responsible for them. On the other hand, any individuals of whom no record has been made will be registered only after a very detailed interrogation.

Inhabitants from the rural areas who wish to join the strategic hamlets will be permitted to do so. With our assistance, they will carry with them all their means of subsistence. In this manner, we can continue to add to the number of persons controlled and protected. The difference in their manner of life, especially with respect to the degree of security accorded to the inhabitants in the protected perimeters, will constitute a powerful attraction throughout the intermediate area. Whenever and wherever we have enough troops and the necessary means, we must create new strategic hamlets.

Only if we approach the problem methodically can we continue to establish a strict control over all the population and its means of subsistence.

The supplying of the bands will become more and more difficult in the intermediate area as we proceed to drain off their means of support. If they can escape the frequent police operations of the interval troops, they will have to maintain themselves in their refuge area under difficult conditions. Armed with considerable information about the enemy (bivouacs, caches, depots, etc.), the sector commander will be able, with additional help on a temporary basis, to follow him into his refuge with good chances of destroying him.

Methodical and patient conduct of operations will, in the easier sectors and those of medium difficulty, lead to the destruction of the enemy's combat apparatus and the restoration of peace within a reasonable length of time.

Offense—Zone Level

If the action of the sector commanders is decisively carried out, the general commanding the zone (department) can move ahead with the essential role of achieving the methodic destruction of the enemy organization over a broader area.

For each sector, he will initially designate the points to be occupied in the execution of an over-all plan to avoid the strangulation of the department. He will especially determine the thoroughfares to be kept open to traffic.

Having dealt the adversary his initial setback, the commanding general takes the offensive. First he attacks the enemy organization in the important towns of the department, especially in the principal town, to put an end to the spectacular terrorist attacks which build the enemy's prestige.

He gives detailed orders for the conduct of police operations. He sees to it that the organization and control of the entire population is secured without delay. He assures that the methods and procedures used are the same throughout the area of the zone to maintain a uniformity of action. He will at all times have at his disposition a significant reserve element to bring pressure to bear on those points which, in their turn, appear most likely to hasten the execution of the pacification plan he has drawn up.

As we have seen, units of the enemy organization rarely coincide with the peacetime administrative boundaries our military organization must adopt.

The sector commanders ought not to stop any action at their own sector limits, but should rather follow up methodically and relentlessly throughout the whole territory of the *enemy* organization attacked—sector or region. Hence, there is a necessity for coordinating operations at the zone level, and for strict planning of methods and procedures.

Refuge areas are usually in irregular terrain to which access is difficult, country often cut through with administrative boundaries. In such a case, the attack on the refuge areas will be launched by the general commanding the zone and at such time as the peripheral police operations of the sector commanders have been concluded.

While he leaves a broad area of initiative to his subordinates, the commanding general assures through frequent inspections that his orders are being strictly followed. He makes sure that his plan of pacification is followed in all areas, especially with respect to practical projects that call for considerable expenditures and in which no waste should occur. Such projects include construction of new roads, or the repair of those that have been sabotaged; construction of new strategic hamlets to receive people fall-ing back from the danger areas; school construction, and economic development of the department to give displaced persons means of subsistence.

A well-conceived plan, executed with determination, courage, and foresight, will save from needless distress a population that will have had more than its share of suffering.

In areas of difficult access, where the guerrilla has been able to estab-lish well-equipped bases for his bands and where he has numbers of seasoned fighters, the sector troops will generally not have sufficient resources to attack and destroy them. They will therefore have to appeal to the intervention troops.

The intervention troops of the zone will, in principle, consist of the zone commander's reserve elements, which can be reinforced by levies on the general reserve of the theater commander if necessary. It is through the judicious use of intervention troops—injecting them at the desired moment at specific points—that the commanding general of the zone will be able to accelerate the process of pacification.

Their normal mission will be the destruction of the armed bands when the interval troops of the sectors have forced them to withdraw into the refuge area. An operation against the bands will not differ essentially from operations conducted by interval troops in the intermediate area. It will be their logical extension.

The number of troops to be employed will depend on the importance of the armed bands to be subdued and the extent of the refuge area. In general, two or three intervention regiments, working closely with inter-val units of the interested sectors, will suffice. They may be commanded by either the zone general or his deputy or, on occasion, by the sector commander most directly interested in the operation.

At an early stage, the target area is sealed off by interval troops of the sectors involved, who will establish themselves in the inhabited rural zones. If the police operation has been properly executed, contact between the guerrillas and the populace will have been broken; the inhab-itants will already be regrouped and organized and an intelligence ser-vice created.

The troops responsible for the isolation of the refuge area will become thoroughly familiar with the terrain over which they repeatedly travel. This sealing-off, or encircling, will not be linear, but will extend over a deep and perfectly well-known zone in which any element of the band will be immediately detected and attacked.

After the net has been put in place, the zone intervention troops will invest—by helicopter, air-drop, or on foot—the entire refuge area, simultaneously if possible. If a band is encountered, the troops must at all times be prepared to engage it, to maneuver, and to destroy it.

The commander of the operation divides the zone up among his units, which will in turn set up light bases maintained by a reserve element. During the course of the first day, the units will prudently and securely fan out as far from their base as they possibly can, to reconnoiter as many as possible of the paths and tracks where, at nightfall, ambushes will be set.

A reserve to be moved by helicopter is held in readiness for disposition by the zone commander, to permit him to exploit and pursue to a finish any engagement at any point in the operational area. Helicopters and light observation aircraft are precious instruments of reconnaissance and protection.

All inhabitants encountered are immediately assembled. The police operation, initiated without delay, will permit the completion of information on depots, bivouacs, caches, hospitals, etc.

The information obtained is exploited on the spot, but carefully and with sufficient troops to avoid surprise by an adversary who is well armed, hardened, and determined to defend himself.

Individuals recognized as part of the enemy organization are arrested and kept within the units for exploitation during the operation.

The population, usually not very numerous, is evacuated entirely to a regroupment center previously set up for this purpose.

From the very beginning, therefore, the bands will be cut off from any contact with the population, and thrown back solely on their own resources.

All troops engaged in the operation have their evening meal before the end of the hours of daylight. After nightfall, no fires are lit. At appropriate points selected during the day, the ambushes go into effect. During the first days after the commencement of the operation, an ambush may take a platoon. But in the days that follow, taking advantage of the disarray of the adversary and our improved knowledge of the terrain, the number of ambush points will increase and the strength of each will diminish to where it does not exceed four or five men.

All paths, in particular those where it is impossible to establish ambushes, are booby-trapped in a simple manner—with grenades or plastic explosives—and retrieved in the morning by the same men who put them in place, to obviate blunders.

At night, the intervention troops and sector troops spread out a vast net; guerrillas who want to move about by night, leave the danger zone, or regroup, will run into it.

In general, it is recommended to fire without warning on any individual who wanders within close range of an ambush, say within ten yards. It is difficult to fire accurately at a greater distance at night, and guerrillas will never appear in front of an ambush in a compact group.

The net is kept in effect for two hours after daybreak, because quite often it is in the morning that guerrillas who want to escape will take their chances.

Around the area and in as great depth as possible, all outposts should keep on the alert, in a position to control all suspicious persons. Any individual not carrying his census card will be considered suspect and arrested.

Inside the zone during the day, patrols search the brush unceasingly and with minute care. They collect the dead for identification, the wounded for interrogation. Prisoners are subjected to quick interrogations and their statements checked on the spot.

This action will compel the guerrillas, cut off from the population and with no knowledge of the situation, to leave their comfortable hiding places—where otherwise they might be discovered—to obtain water or food or to attempt to flee. Their wounded will become an impossible burden.

Appropriate psychological action, using loudspeakers or leaflets, will quite likely secure the surrender of weak individuals whom circumstances have placed beyond the reach and authority of their chiefs. Many of the guerrillas who have escaped the ambushes will give themselves up, demoralized. The entire operation must last as long as is necessary to destroy the guerrilla band completely.

Anything that would facilitate the existence of the guerrillas in any way, or which could conceivably be used by them—depots, shelters, caches, food, crops, houses, etc.—must be systematically destroyed or brought in. This will actually permit the methodical recovery of materiel and food, which can be distributed to the regrouped civilians. All inhabitants and livestock must be evacuated from the refuge area.

When they leave, the intervention troops must not only have completely destroyed the bands, but must leave behind them an area empty of all resources and absolutely uninhabitable.

The operation against the armed bands in a refuge area, supported by intervention troops, should spell the end of the battle against the guerrilla in a sector. To be successful, it must be prepared in the greatest detail at the echelon of the general commanding the zone. It should get under way when the operations of the interval troops in the sectors have created a favorable situation and the zone commander has assembled all the necessary men and materiel. Then, carefully prepared and energetically carried out, it cannot fail.

Once successful, the sector commander will be able to regroup and control all of the inhabitants of his sector—the ultimate aim of *modern warfare* operations.

However, organization and control of the population, and supplementary controls over food, circulation of persons and goods, animals, etc., as well as a flawless intelligence service, must remain in force until peace has been restored to the entire national territory. Any lack of vigilance or premature dismantling of the control system will certainly permit the enemy to recoup lost ground and jeopardize the peace of the sector.

Offense—Theater Level

The commander-in-chief of the entire theater of operations should maintain a considerable general reserve. This will permit him to strike at the precise time and place he judges opportune in the conduct of theater-level operations. By judicious employment of reserves, as we have seen, he will be able to accelerate and bring about the pacification of difficult areas.

For reasons of troop economy, certain areas may be abandoned or held by only very small forces. Here, the enemy will be able to organize and maintain significant forces. When the theater commander decides on their pacification, the normal resources of the sector and zone may be inadequate. Such operations will therefore fall to units of the general reserve.

At the beginning of any conflict, the enemy normally will not be able to launch hostilities simultaneously throughout the entire territory. He first sets himself up in areas favorable to guerrilla warfare and attempts to keep these under his control.

At this point, forceful action, quickly begun and vigorously carried out according to the principles discussed, ought to annihilate the guerrilla and prevent extension of the conflict, The success of such an operation is of the utmost importance, because it can re-establish the peace in short order.

In any case, the operational area must be clearly defined and isolated. Initially, this is the role of the zones and sectors nearest the enemy. At the first aggressive acts, elements of the forces of order already in place—the army, gendarmerie, police, various peacetime intelligence services—attempt to determine as accurately as possible the limits of the area under the enemy's control.

After quickly establishing the limits of this area, the measures previously studied—control and organization of the populace, creation of an efficient intelligence service—can contain the enemy's sphere of action even further. The extent of this final restriction of enemy activity will delimit the area of attack.

The number of the troops (two to four divisions, if one accepts the Korean experience), the civilian and military means to be committed, the need for strict coordination of complex actions—all means that a theater-level operation ought not to be launched until detailed study permits the drawing up of a precise plan of action when the necessary men and equipment have been assembled. Insufficient means or carelessness of preparation and execution of operations will lead to certain failure; the area of the conflict would spread, and a long war could not be avoided.

The commander of the operation should be the commander of the general reserve units to be used. His will be the complete responsibility not merely to weaken the bands or disperse them, but rather to destroy the combat apparatus of the enemy and re-establish normal life within the affected area.

No time limit for the operation should be set ahead of time. It will end when the enemy's combat organization—guerrilla bands included—are completely destroyed (that is, when not one more guerrilla remains in the region), and when a cohesive system capable of preventing any offensive return of the adversary has been established.

At the appropriate time, after the general reserves have been withdrawn, an assistant can be charged with assuring a rapid return to peacetime conditions in the liberated territory with whatever means are available and with the organization that has been created.

Although a theater-level operation differs in size from those previously considered, the principles to be applied are the same.

If the number of troops available can cover the whole target area, operations should begin simultaneously in both the intermediate and refuge areas. Valuable time may thus be saved. But we can only rarely bring together the troops necessary for an operation of such size.

Therefore, the operation usually begins in the intermediate area—which borders the refuge area—the importance of which we have already described, and with whose character we are familiar.

A vast police operation covering this whole area will enable us to destroy the important politico-military organism implanted there, and to complete if necessary the destruction of the politico-administrative organization of the towns.

At times we will run across guerrilla bands, which we will attempt to destroy, but above all we must put an end to their free passage and oblige them to withdraw and live in the refuge areas.

Parallel to the police operation, the now familiar organization is created to control food, animals, circulation of persons and consumer goods, etc. The inhabitants are regrouped in strategic hamlets, which will be equipped with the necessary means to ensure their control and protection. Villages, roads, and outposts are set up and a normal administration created.

The inhabited rural area will in this way become an immense worksite in which the populace, properly harnessed, can render precious and effective assistance.

It is only when the rural area operation has ended that theater-level operation against the refuge areas can be undertaken.

Our intelligence services, the civilian population, and prisoners, as well as the impression of strength emanating from a vast operation forcefully and methodically conducted, will have enabled us, before the launching of the operation, to be well-informed about the bands—their weapons, numbers, usual bivouac areas, shelters, caches, depots, normal routes of movement, means of subsistence, and sources of information.

We will not approach the refuge areas blindly, but will first have completely and precisely blueprinted our objectives.

Although it is on a much larger scale, the theater-level operation is carried out just like those against the refuge areas of the sector and the zone.

After first setting up a blockade, every modern method of transportation—helicopter, parachute, etc.—is employed simultaneously in the shortest possible time, to clamp down on the entire enemy refuge area. The guerrilla bands are allowed no opportunity to escape.

The entire operation lasts long enough for them to be destroyed. It ends only when the area they have chosen as their haven is wiped clean of all means of subsistence and rendered completely useless to them.

Thus, we shall have achieved a real specialization of the troops used in *modern warfare.*

The grid units are the first troops used, to stop the adversary's offensive effort. Responsible for occupying towns and sensitive points throughout the country and for ensuring the security of the main roads, their apparently static mission should be the most active.

Their role is quite important because they partition off the enemy area, stop the extension of the territory he controls, and, thanks to the outposts they occupy and the network of roads they keep open, provide excellent bases of departure for troops specialized in offensive operations.

Their responsibility extends not only to the safety of the cities, but also to the security of the immense majority of the population living in medium-sized and small towns. This security depends upon the ability of the checkerboard units to destroy the enemy's organization in the towns, to set up an effective control system among the populace to control the movement of persons and goods, on which will depend in large part the success of operations conducted on the periphery by the interval units.

The grid troops must be trained in police operations. These they should carry out firmly, but with tact and discretion, not to alienate themselves unnecessarily from the people with whom they will be in permanent contact.

They will be replaced little by little with normal police forces, in particular the gendarmerie, once the assistance and collaboration of the people has been acquired. Then they will go to reinforce the interval units and permit them to extend their field of activity.

The interval units should be composed of excellent, well-trained troops. Their basic mission is to destroy the enemy's politico-military organization in the intermediate area of their sector, to regroup the dispersed populace to ensure their protection, and to organize them so that the inhabitants participate in their own defense.

These troops will be nomads, capable of living away from their base for long periods, of dispersing over a great area to carry out police operations in depth, and of quickly regrouping in the event of an engagement with the enemy so that they can maneuver and destroy the guerrilla bands.

The intervention units are elite troops who will seek out the bands in their refuge areas and destroy them.

To follow a resolute adversary in difficult terrain, to move long distances on foot by day and night to reach him, to man ambushes all night long in small teams of four or five men along forest paths—all this calls for excellent training and insuperable morale.

Cadres of the highest quality are needed to conduct an effective police operation, to interrogate interesting prisoners quickly at the very point of their capture, and to exploit the situation without losing any time. This difficult and costly training will be available to only a small number of units. They should be utilized judiciously so that they do not suffer unnecessary wear and tear.

If one accepts the Korean experience and the present needs of the war in Algeria, the commanding general of an important theater of operations ought to have at least four divisions at his disposal.

Consolidated under the command of a dynamic leader, well up on the combat procedures of *modern warfare,* they will be capable of successfully handling within a few months the most threatened and vulnerable areas.

To sum up, guerrilla warfare, because of the advantages that accrue to the guerrilla—for example, the terrain he has chosen and the population that supports him—can be effectively conducted by small bands against a much larger army. The guerrilla's adversary is always at arm's length; the guerrilla's numerous agents can continually observe him, and at their leisure study his vulnerable points. The guerrilla bands will always be able to choose the propitious moment to attack and harass their opponents.

To be effective, his operations do not call for coordination of all his elements, which are too widely dispersed even though they operate on the same territory. Audacity, initiative, courage—these are the chief qualities of guerrilla leaders. In the beginning, at least, guerrilla warfare is a war of lieutenants and young captains.

We on the contrary attack an enemy who is invisible, fluid, uncatchable. In order to get to him, we have no alternative but to throw a net of fine mesh over the entire area in which the bands move. Counterguerrilla operations therefore cannot succeed unless they are conducted on a large scale, unless they last the necessary length of time, and unless they are prepared and directed in greatest detail.

To the words of Colonel Beebe, already cited above, "A counterguerrilla operation ends only when there are no more guerrillas in the area, and not when the guerrilla has been disorganized and dispersed," let me add, "and when the enemy's entire warfare organization has been destroyed and ours put in its place."

The struggle against the guerrilla is not, as one might suppose, a war of lieutenants and captains. The number of troops that must be put in action, the vast areas over which they will be led to do battle, the necessity of coordinating diverse actions over these vast areas, the politico-military measures to be taken regarding the populace, the necessarily close cooperation with various branches of the civil administration—all this requires that operations against the guerrilla be conducted according to a plan, established at a very high command level,[2] capable at any moment of making quick, direct intercession effectively felt in the wide areas affected by *modern warfare.*

The counterguerrilla struggle is definitely a question of method. A modern state possesses forces sufficiently large to fight him. Our repeated failures result solely from poor employment of our resources.

Many military leaders judge these insufficient. We know of no example in military history of a soldier who went into battle with all the means he thought he needed. The great military leader is the one who knows how to win with the means at his disposal.

NOTES

1. Translator's note: In French administrative parlance an *igame* is an *inspecteur général d'administration en mission extraordinaire,* e.g., an official outranking several departmental prefects and supervising them. The territory under his control is then known as an *igamie.*

2. In principle, that of the commander of the theater of operations.

Part Three

CARRYING THE WAR TO THE ENEMY

Chapter 11

THE INADEQUACIES
OF TRADITIONAL WARFARE

We have just studied ways to react against an opponent employing the methods of *modern warfare* on our own territory. But the means prescribed provide only for the destruction of forces the enemy has introduced or organized within our frontiers.

The enemy, however, before moving to open warfare, will attempt to assure himself of the support of one or more friendly, nonbelligerent foreign nations. There, he will set up important bases for training his troops and will install reserves of war materiel. This territory will very often serve as a base of departure for attacks launched into our territory. It is there that the enemy will, at the opening of hostilities, set up his command structure, and will shape it gradually into the provisional government he hopes to set up on our territory as soon as there is a large enough area conquered.

The fact that the state which supports our adversaries is a nonbelligerent one seems to place these bases beyond our range and leave the enemy completely free to receive without interruption the men and materiel that will permit him to supply his battle on our territory.

As long as this considerable war potential is not destroyed or neutralized, peace, even if completely restored within our own borders, will be precarious and in continual jeopardy.

The enemy's freedom of action beyond our frontiers is one of the factors determining the duration of the conflict. Material support and the assurance of strong and continuing aid from abroad are essential to maintaining a high morale among those fighting in our interior. Without external aid and the hope of an Allied landing, most of the French maquis under the occupation would not have been able to hold out under the pressure of the German attacks. And several more recent examples also demonstrate the importance that the support of a nonbelligerent state in *modern warfare* can have on the outcome of a conflict.

Greece was unable to crush the Communist attack until Yugoslavia, having left the Soviet camp, no longer served as a support base to the armed bands fighting on Greek soil. The principal error of the French in Indochina was not to have made enough of an effort to gain a victory before the arrival of Chinese Communists at the Tonkin frontier. From then on, the Vietminh were able to make use of important bases in China, where they could freely provision themselves and where their large units could be formed and trained. The character of the war immediately changed. It was lost for the French, who were no longer capable of supplying, so far from home, a theater of operations that had so increased in complexity.

The destruction or neutralization of enemy bases on foreign territory is essential if we are to hasten the end of hostilities and ensure a durable peace.

The simplest solution is to obtain diplomatic assurances that neighboring states will not contribute assistance to the enemy. But since the Spanish Civil War, in particular, different ideologies have divided the great world powers into opposed camps. Our ideological opponents will, under various guises, give our enemies greater or lesser aid, according to their capabilities and their geographic situation, but, in any case, they will support them.

Moreover, by the very fact of the present interdependence of nations, any revolutionary movement in any country will be exploited by others for their own ends. The Soviet bloc, in particular, will do everything possible to feed a conflict susceptible of weakening the opposing camp. The enemy will undoubtedly seek support in a country where diplomatic action will have no chance of success.

When diplomatic intervention proves ineffective, attempts will be made to establish along the frontiers of the territory under attack a system capable of depriving the enemy of delivery of support from without. But the boundaries of a state are long and ways of crossing them plentiful.

In a defensive endeavor of this kind, the task of the navy is to guard the sea frontiers. Guided by an effective intelligence service, it is able to intercept suspect ships, even on the high seas. Its action can thus considerably interfere with the enemy's supplies. But this will not succeed in cutting off contraband in arms and other war materiel indispensable to him. To keep a close watch on the ports and coasts is the responsibility of the civil authority. But this involves great problems because of the number of administrative areas concerned, and because of the volume of the traffic to be controlled, particularly in the large ports. Also, rigorous regulation delays a country's own supplies and for this reason is not practical.

By day, the air force can ensure the effective surveillance of land and sea frontiers, and can even attack enemy supply convoys when they cross the frontier. At night, however, its role is much reduced. It cannot stop parachute drops of materiel or agents, not even in closely watched areas, which can escape our control for sufficiently long periods.

Guarding the frontiers on the ground is even more difficult to realize. We know that guerrillas use essentially light war materiel and use it sparingly. Even if we succeed in cutting off their main penetration routes, there are still the little mountain paths known only to experts. We can rarely cut them off entirely.

Even the fortified perimeter along the edge of the Tonkin delta, established at great cost by General de Lattre in 1950–51, did not succeed in impeding regular exchanges between the Vietminh units infiltrated into the delta. They continued to receive all their military provisions from the outside, and saw to it that their comrades, installed around the perimeter or in the Upper Region, got their needed rations of rice. We were never able to stop that traffic.

In Algeria, drawing on past experience, we have managed to set up a fragile, but tight, barrier of indisputable effectiveness. If our opponents are stalemated, if they have not been successful in creating guerrilla units larger than company size, it is in large part because the border fence has not permitted them to receive the supplies vital to the normal development of their activities. The guerrilla operates sporadically, intending more to maintain his hold over the rural population than to disturb the forces of order. It is therefore more toward terrorism in the cities that they have bent their efforts, principally because this type of action calls for a minimum of materiel.

This is why hostilities in Algeria are stalled. The adversary is counting on the proven inability of France to pursue a costly and seemingly interminable conflict, permitting him ultimately to attain his war aims.

But the barrier possesses the serious defect of all defensive organizations. There is no secret about its location; the enemy can observe it functioning and detect its weaknesses.

At irregular intervals, sporadic attacks in small force, never pressed to a culmination, are enough to immobilize large numbers of troops. Moreover, the ease with which these forays can be repulsed develops a false sense of security, which can be very dangerous. We must never permit ourselves to be decoyed. The enemy will profit from these repeated forays to maintain the offensive spirit of their troops and to study our reactions. Only when they have assembled the necessary men and materiel to force the barrier will they really attack.

The lesson of Dien Bien Phu should not be forgotten. The camp's entrenched garrison believed itself secure behind its extensive barbed-wire network, which in some places ran more than fifty yards in depth. The troops readily looked forward to a mass enemy attack, which they thought themselves capable of easily repulsing. By the time their attack was finally unleashed, the Vietminh had had plenty of time to appreciate the true value of the defensive system, and they brought together the means necessary for a breakthrough.

No doubt the barrier has a certain value, but it has no effect on the combat potential the enemy can rally together with impunity along the frontiers.

Formerly, particularly during the nineteenth century, when armed bands crossed the frontier of French overseas possessions they were followed. If necessary, the country giving them refuge was attacked and quite often brought to submission. Agreements among a few of the great powers were sufficient to localize a conflict, usually a simple incident our army had the capability of quickly concluding. Today, because of the power of international organizations and the intricacies of world problems, this kind of intervention would lead to reactions throughout the entire world, and certainly to an unpredictable extension of the conflict.

But follow-up action remains the normal reflex of the traditional military man. Actually, if enemy bases outside our territory are close to the frontiers, sometimes within range of our heavier weapons, they are a tempting target, certainly easy to reach and destroy. Let us consider the effects of an air attack against these bases and a traditional attack by ground forces supported by aviation and artillery.

An air attack offers the advantage of secret preparation and rapid execution. It will, however, have decisive results only if it is massive. Therefore, it requires considerable resources. There is an element of surprise only during the first bombardments; dispersion and then camouflage quickly make them less profitable. Despite precise information, targets will be progressively more difficult to define. They will often be located close to built-up areas, which must bear the brunt of the bombardments.

Finally, aerial attacks do not permit the realization of desired objectives. They accord our enemies complete freedom to present the facts in the manner most favorable to them—the number of civilian victims are considerably exaggerated and the military results minimized. A bombing run is transformed by unfavorable propaganda into a terrorist raid that the enemy press can exploit. Even a large part of the French press exploited the only bombing attack the French Army in Algeria ever carried out—the one in February, 1958, on the F.L.N. base of Sakhiet Sidi Youssef, near the Tunisian frontier.

A conventional attack against enemy bases by ground forces also presents disadvantages. The fact is that the crossing of the frontier of a state by a regularly constituted army is a *casus belli*. It is equivalent to a declaration of war, and international usage would definitely designate us as the aggressor.

Modern warfare has not been codified. Innumerable attacks can be committed in a country by a powerful enemy combat force; armed bands based abroad can regularly cross a frontier and harass the army of a neighboring country in order to overthrow its regime—and none of these is a *casus belli*. Terrorists and armed bands can always be deceptive to the eyes of observers uneducated to the conditions of *modern warfare,* or to persons who are merely of bad faith. But the traditional army with its great numbers of troops, its heavy materiel, slow to move about and impossible to hide, can never pass unobserved.

A ground attack in sufficient strength, carried out with determination, would most certainly produce initial good results. Most of the storage points situated near our frontiers could be destroyed or captured; a significant portion of the enemy forces could be annihilated or captured, but never all of them. Adept at guerrilla warfare, elements we cannot attack or which have succeeded in fleeing, benefiting from the support of the people to whom we appear as the aggressor, would find refuge in areas inaccessible to our heavy equipment.

Without gaining any decisive advantage, we would considerably widen the dimensions of a battlefield we already find difficult to manage. But, above all, we would give the enemy unexpected support on the international plane, support awaiting only a favorable occasion to manifest itself openly against us.

If it is indispensable to destroy these bases abroad that are essential to our enemies, it is certainly not methods of traditional warfare we should employ. Attacked on our own territory with the methods of *modern warfare,* we must carry the war to the enemy with the same methods.

Chapter 12

MODERN WARFARE IN ENEMY TERRITORY

Traditional warfare methods interfere to a certain extent with our opponents' supplies, but cannot halt them.

The conventional army, as we have seen, deploys its considerable resources on a field of battle devoid of the enemy. It cannot meet him except by chance, because the two normally operate on completely different planes, and the army's attacks fall more often than not into a void.

It is accepted that the final stake of *modern warfare* is the control of the populace. The army should therefore make its main effort in those areas where the population is densest; that is, in the cities. But in Algeria, after a few spectacular early successes (the battle of Algiers in 1957), the large cities were abandoned to enemy terrorist organizations, while the main troop units chased after small and unimportant bands in unpopulated regions.[1]

(It should be stressed that this recurring error springs from the fact that the army by tradition rejects the use of the *modern warfare* methods it little understands. On the other hand, the violence of attacks the army has undergone in certain intellectual circles, and the poor backing it has received from the government, have certainly not encouraged it to involve itself in operations for which it is in any case poorly prepared.)

Attacked on our own territory, we must first defend ourselves. Then we may carry the war to the enemy and grant them no respite until they capitulate. We will attack them on their terrain with weapons of *modern warfare* that will permit us to strike directly, in their territory, without exposing ourselves to the international complications the employment of traditional arms would surely evoke.

The conduct of *modern warfare* requires close collaboration with the population. We must first assure ourselves of its support. Experience has demonstrated that it is by no means necessary to enjoy the sympathy of the majority of the people to obtain their backing; most are amorphous, indifferent. We will limit ourselves to forming an active elite and introducing it as leaven into the mass to produce action at the desired moment.

We need cadres first, and they are easy to find. (In the former French Union, a number of men remained devoted; this was amply demonstrated in Indochina, and later in Algeria.) They are doubtless more attracted by the benefits they expect than by our country itself, but this attachment can be unflagging if we are resolved to accept it and are firm in our intentions and objectives. We know also that, in troubled periods, self-interest and ambition have always been powerful incentives for dynamic individuals who want to move out of their rut and get somewhere. Self-interest and ambition can be consistent with an ideal and with honorable intentions. It is this ideal and these intentions that we must discover. In each country, within each race, in every social stratum, we must find a reason, an idea, often different ones in neighboring areas, but capable nonetheless of constituting adequate motivation for the assumption of necessary risks. The present troubled period, with its social and ideological struggles, provides a broad field for research through which we can find the basic elements appropriate to our undertaking.

As every state, every political system has its opponents and internal enemies, so will the regime we want to destroy. Their numbers are always large in a nation occupied by foreign troops, under a dictatorial regime, and in certain outlying regions where popular opposition to the central power has not disappeared.

It is among these that we will find the cadres we need.

ESTABLISHMENT OF MAQUIS ZONES

The installation of advance elements on enemy territory requires a prior study in depth to determine the areas into which we ought to direct our efforts. The study should gather information on the physical, economic, and human geography; the current psychological climate, and the disposition of military and police forces. This study will permit us to determine which areas will be more responsive to our action and where the conduct of a large operation can be most effective.

At first, our resources will be very limited. We must therefore choose the least protected areas—sparsely populated mountain regions, for example, where secrecy can be maintained for the time needed to plant our contact teams. Our action begins with the establishment of maquis zones on foreign territory.

Experience has shown that in an area suited to the setting up of a maquis team, there is no room for two masters—the land belongs to the first occupant. Accordingly, it is very difficult to dislodge the people already living there. The rugged life led by the maquis, the fear they must inspire among the surrounding inhabitants in order to subsist, will oblige the natives to support them despite themselves. In those areas where we intend to begin, we must become the primary force, to prevent the rise of any authority other than our own.

For taking over a particular maquis zone, we recruit initial cadres and, if possible, a leader to take over the area command who will be representative of the ethnic and geographic group predominant in that zone.

The cadres should be from the area in question and know it perfectly, in order to be able to make recruiting contacts with men who will be entrusted with creating the assembly areas of future maquis teams. They should all be local people or persons who have maintained friendly connections or family relationships.

The Contact Teams

These first volunteers will be assembled in a special camp for training contact teams. Following a process of rigorous selection, they will be classified into three categories—combat personnel (about 50 per cent of the volunteers), communications specialists (25 per cent), and political and intelligence agents (25 per cent).

Their training will consist of basic general instruction (political, psychological, military, paratroop, counterintelligence) and specialized instruction (in particular, communications). This training will be conducted by specialized volunteer cadres, officers, and N.C.O.'s, who will ultimately assume charge of the maquis bands when they are activated.

At the end of the first training period, lasting two or three months depending on the intellectual capacity of the pupils, the first contact missions will be constituted. They will generally be composed of a team leader and his assistant (taken from among those who received the specialized instruction for combat personnel), a communications specialist (voice), and two political and intelligence agents. About ten such teams will suffice to prospect the maquis zone and to make the contacts necessary for creating bases. The other volunteers will continue their training, especially the wireless operators, whose instruction must be especially thorough.

At the right moment, the contact teams will be assembled together in the maquis zone. This will be accomplished by night parachute drops, or by infiltration by land or water. Night drops of small teams by trained air crews offer the advantage of great secrecy and spare the men both a long difficult trek and the risks of interception.

Each team is independent and operates in the vicinity of a village that is well known to at least one of the agents and in which it will be possible to renew friendly connections and make desirable contacts. Radio communication will enable the work of the teams to be monitored.

When the contact mission is well under way, the team leader and an intelligence agent return to base, usually by a land route.[2] By this time, they should be familiar enough with the terrain not to run any risk. They will take along with them a few picked young people, already given some basic training, to enroll them in the maquis commando. The assistant team leader, the communications specialist, and an intelligence agent remain in the area so that contacts are maintained and, if possible, improved. This phase of taking up positions and making contacts should last from one to two months.

Information furnished by the contact teams, coordinated upon the return of the team leaders, will enable the officer commanding the maquis to follow the evolution of the situation. It enables him to direct the recruitment and training of the necessary personnel, particularly that of the maquis command, which should consist of about 100 men. He can coordinate radio contact with the teams remaining in the field. He will be able to set the precise limits of future maquis zones, designate and study parachute drop areas, and establish quotas for weapons, radios, and other materiel.

When all the equipment has been mustered, when the training of the commando group, the team leaders, and the various specialists is completed, when the organization of the zone is fully coordinated, an effective maquis should be set to work as soon as possible.

The maquis team chiefs are parachuted first. Upon their arrival, they will organize their maquis teams for personal protection. Maquis action begins immediately with the dismantling of the local administration. The maquis leader follows his commando unit and radio equipment. He establishes himself as the ultimate authority in his area and puts an end to any action of the local police or gendarmerie that interferes with his activity. A few well-calculated acts of sabotage and terrorism will then compel any reluctant citizens to give the required cooperation. Harassment of communication lines can begin, which will lead to the isolation of the maquis zone. By means of internal subversion, insecurity can be sowed in the surrounding villages.

Once this important phase is complete, the development and extension of the maquis zone will depend on the leader and the reactions of the enemy. Effective weapon strength should rapidly reach 1,000 rifles. Experience has shown that a maquis team of 1,000 armed men, supported by 2,000 or 3,000 collaborating inhabitants, is practically invulnerable to the police forces.

If several maquis efforts are launched at the same time, they can create disturbances of incalculable magnitude in the enemy's country of support.

Other quicker and more brutal techniques can be employed. One used in Indochina led to the installation of 20,000 organized and equipped partisans in the Upper Region of Tonking and in Laos in a single year. This figure was to be increased to 50,000 in the autumn of 1954, which would have permitted the soundly based reconquest of Upper Tonking, the haunt of large Vietminh units. Unfortunately, this action, undertaken on the initiative of General de Lattre de Tassigny, came too late. The regrettable Dien Bien Phu incident brought the sudden cessation of hostilities and prevented us from exploiting our opportunities in depth.

The action of French maquis teams did, however, permit the evacuation without losses of the fortified camp of Nasan; the reconquest by Laos of the provinces of Phong-Saly and Sam-Neua without the help of regular troops; the total interdiction of the direct road from Lao-Kay to Dien Bien Phu for the entire duration of the siege, as well as the immobilization of more than fourteen battalions of the Vietminh regular army on Route R.P. 41, the umbilical cord of the besiegers; the recovery of hundreds of prisoners, etc.

And yet, the establishment of maquis in the Tonkinese Upper Region, right in the middle of an area under Vietminh control, seemed a gamble when it was undertaken in 1952. This potential of the maquis command, although scarcely noticed at the time and already forgotten, ought not be lost sight of.

Once large maquis teams are installed, we undertake action in the towns. The maquis zones will serve as assembly areas and as refuge areas for forces charged with creating a feeling of insecurity in the small surrounding towns.

The large towns and cities in themselves constitute maquis zones. The extent of their surface area, their population density, the difficulty of establishing there a strict control over a large and concentrated population, will permit our agents to set themselves up, to organize, and to create a reign of insecurity sufficient to cause the authorities considerable trouble.

Concealing the Build-up

In order to succeed, our action in enemy territory has to be carried out with discretion. We must recruit, assemble, and train our maquis elements in absolute secrecy. A camp capable of training 500 men, located in an isolated area of difficult access, will serve our needs.

The most practical method, the one guaranteeing the best results, is to turn over a frontier sector command to whoever is designated to prepare and conduct the necessary action. The regular sector forces would continue their usual tasks during the maquis training period and would be in a position to support them when action begins.

In no case do regular troops, elements of regular troops, or isolated nationals cross the frontier. Our intervention troops will receive only enemy weapons and equipment, captured in combat or otherwise procured. Many of our maquis will be recruited directly from among the enemy, especially from among prisoners, and natives of the territory where our action takes place.

Thus, we will have carried the war onto foreign territory without using regular troops. With respect to international opinion, the movement we launch may be presented by ourselves and our friends as an internal uprising, from which we are apparently divorced but which nonetheless has our official sympathy. We will attempt to give the military action a clearly defined political character and, if possible, a symbolic leader to represent it. We will give it any assistance that will contribute to its development, in anticipation of the moment when the international situation permits us to give aid officially.

Certainly our opponents won't be deceived; they will know from where the blows are coming. But their protests will carry no more weight than our own. *Modern warfare,* not having been codified, remains officially ignored. Any diplomatic intervention would look like meddling in the internal affairs of a sovereign country and would be rejected.

Peace may then be re-established only on our own terms; that is, when the aid given to our enemies has ceased.

NOTES

1. The disturbances of December, 1960, in the larger Algerian towns were the result of such abandonment, which tended to worsen the entire problem.

2. Or by helicopter, a considerable saving in time.

CONCLUSION

In *modern warfare,* as in the traditional wars of the past, it is absolutely essential to make use of all the weapons the enemy employs. Not to do so would be absurd.

We lost the war in Indochina largely because we hesitated to take the necessary measures or took them too late. For the same reason we are going to lose the war in Algeria. France will seek a compromise peace it never would have considered if the army had given it the victory the country had rightly come to expect in view of the sacrifices it had made.

If an army has atomic weapons and is firmly resolved to use them to dissuade a potential enemy from attacking, we ought equally to be firmly decided to employ every resource of *modern warfare* to ensure our protection.

Such resolution, clearly stated, may be enough to deter aggression.

The forms of warfare and its weapons have evolved gradually over the ages. We are once again at an important juncture of that evolution.

Science is allowing the military to kill more and more of the enemy at greater and greater distances. Airmen, artillerymen, even infantrymen have killed and been killed without having seen a single enemy. The hard and pitiless realities of war—cruel and brutal physical contact with the enemy—are being spared the modern soldier. Combatants philosophically accept killing and dying, but usually avoid the rugged contact of physical suffering and death individually given and received.

With the advent of the atomic weapon, the power of destruction has become such that its use would probably involve the simultaneous disappearance of belligerents of both camps. It will therefore not be used.

But war itself will not disappear. The increasing power of weaponry, which places distance between combatants, is also abruptly bringing them together. Once again, they will confront one another on a clearly defined field, and will rediscover the physical contact lost these many centuries. Immense armies will no longer simultaneously invade a vast battlefield. War will be a juxtaposition of a multitude of small actions. Intelligence and ruse, allied to physical brutality, will succeed the power of blind armament.

A problem confronts us: Will we in *modern warfare* make use of all necessary resources to win, as we have always done in the traditional wars of the past and as we at present envisage doing when we construct nuclear weapons?

Other soldiers have been confronted with problems of this nature in the course of history. At the battle of Crécy in 1346, the army of the French King refused to use the bow and the arrow the English handled so effectively. For them, true combat, the only fair and permissible kind, remained man-to-man, body-to-body. To use an arrow, to kill one's adversary from afar, was a kind of impermissible cowardliness not compatible with their concepts of honor and chivalry.

At Agincourt in 1415, the lesson of Crécy went unheeded. Once again on horseback, with breastplate and sword, French knights advanced on English archers, and once again were crushed.

The knights, at that time the professional military men of the nation, refused to use the new arms, but the King of France, responsible for the destiny of the country, adopted them and armed his infantry with the bow. Charles VII, in fact, from that time on obliged every parish to maintain an archer, the first step toward our present national army.

Knights, having become an archaic and useless luxury, disappeared from the field of battle. For them, a page of history has been turned for all time.

No nation deprives its army of material resources or moral support. It allows it its own system of justice, swift and severe, to pass judgment in the context of warfare on those soldiers found guilty of offenses or crimes; doctors to care for the wounded on the field of battle; chaplains to ensure spiritual peace to the dying, and the power of life and death over opponents within the framework of the rules of war. Usually, the army lives isolated from the people for the duration of conflict.

The nation does not ask the army to define problems, but to win the war it is engaged in and to ensure the population's protection and security against any threatening danger.

If, like the knights of old, our army refused to employ all the weapons of *modern warfare,* it could no longer fulfill its mission. We would no longer be defended. Our national independence, the civilization we hold dear, our very freedom would probably perish.

INDEX

About The Author

ROGER TRINQUIER (1908-1986) was born into a peasant family and was graduated from the military academy at Saint-Maixent. He was posted in the Far East for much of his career, serving first in Indochina and then in China. Following World War II, he campaigned in Vietnam before returning to organize and train a colonial parachute battalion in France. Then he was reassigned to Indochina as an expert on counterguerrilla warfare. This tour was followed by his active role in the revolt of May 1958 by the French army in Algeria, for which he was labeled "a political colonel". Afterward Colonel Trinquier led a group of fellow officers—recruited from elite units and officially retired, but with the approval of the Ministry of Defense— to serve as mercenaries in Katanga Province, Zaire, under the secessionist leader Moïse Tshombe. He published *La Guerre Moderne*, which was translated into English, and a number of other books dealing with the Indochina war and the exploits of French airborne forces.